ALSO BY FLOCABULARY

Flocabulary: The Hip-Hop Approach to SAT-Level Vocabulary Building

Flocabulary: Hip-Hop U.S. History

ten beats

THE RAPPER'S HANDBOOK

A GUIDE TO FREESTYLING, WRITING RHYMES, AND BATTLING

by Emcee Escher
with Alex Rappaport

Flocabulary Press * New York

www.flocabulary.com

THE RAPPER'S HANDBOOK. Copyright 2006 by Flocabulary, LLC.

All rights reserved under the Pan-American and Internation Copyright Conventions.

No part of this book may be used or reproduced in any manner whatsoever without written permission except in the case of brief quotations embodied in critical articles and reviews. For information, address Flocabulary Press, 315 West 39th Street, Studio 1610, New York, NY 10018.

ISBN: 0-9768292-1-5
ISBN (13 Digit): 978-0-9768292-1-8

www.flocabulary.com

FIRST EDITION

Written by Emcee Escher (Blake Harrison) with Alexander Rappaport
Cover Artwork by Jen Swanson
Design by B. Harrison
Illustrations by Allison van Hée
Printed in the United States

0 1 2 3 4 5 6 7 8 9

"Rap is rhythm and poetry."
- Rakim

Contents

Preface ix

Part One - Freestyling
Guide to Freestyling 3
Cipher Etiquette 101 13
Freestyle Rap Games 16

Part Two - Elevating Your Rhymes
Slant Rhymes 23
Rhyme Scheme 29
In-Rhymes 32
Multies 36
Wordplay 50
Metaphors 57
Vocabulary 68
References 76
Other Techniques 89

Part Three - Performing
Flow 98
The History of Flow 111
Hand Gestures 122
Move the Crowd 136

Part Four - Battling
Guide to Battling 142
Punchlines 160

Part Five - Recording
Setting Up a Project Studio   170
On the Mic   181

Part Six - The Motivation Behind Your Rhymes
Why Spit Rhymes   188
The Cure for Writer's Block   191

Discography and Sources   203

Appendix I - Idioms   209
Appendix II - Rhyming with Famous Names   213
Appendix III - Rhymes for Rhymeless Words   214

Preface

A rapper is a poet with a beat. To rap is to spit, and a rapper spits syncopated words that tell stories, show off, and teach. A rapper is also an emcee, and an emcee moves the crowd. Whether he's rocking a basement party in the Bronx or controlling the mic for thousands of screaming fans at the Superdome, he uses his infectious rhymes to connect with his audience. A rapper is also a lyricist, and a lyricist plays with words. A lyricist crafts complex rhymes full of metaphor, alliteration, in-rhyme, assonance and enough wordplay to make a crossword puzzle dizzy. He flows with stylish ease, dropping knowledge on the beat, behind the beat, or in the pocket, right where he wants to. A rapper is all of these things.

Hip-hop music has come a long way in the past 30 years. From back rooms and block parties in South Bronx in the late seventies to the Golden Age in the late eighties through gangsta rap in the nineties to today, where you can hear emcees rapping all over the world in dozens of languages. In Poland and Italy, in China and Korea, in India and Ghana, in Peru and Columbia, a whole generation has adopted hip-hop as their own. They're not just listening; they're writing rhymes too.

It makes sense. Rap music is the most democratic music in the world, open to anyone with vocal chords.

You don't need a piano or a drum set, or money for guitar lessons. All you need is your voice and a desire to spit. A pad and pen, maybe, but those are optional.

There is no cookie-cutter for rappers, and this book is for everyone out there with a desire to freestyle, write rhymes, or battle. Freestyling and writing rhymes are not only truly thrilling and fun, but they'll also open your mind up in ways you probably never have before. Freestyling and battling involve a quickness of thought that rivals any thinking exercise. Writing involves analytic thinking and creativity. Whether you ever release an album or not, those are skills that you'll use for the rest of your life.

This book is the first comprehensive handbook for rappers. It covers all of the major aspects of rapping, divided into sections. You don't need to read this book straight through. Feel free to skip around, though some of the sections may reference earlier chapters. There is a lot of information here. Don't try to swallow it all at once. Elevating your rhymes takes time and effort. It may be worth it to tackle one section at a time, before moving on. Of course, it's up to you.

This book quotes from various artists including Eminem, Jay-Z, Rakim, Bun B, Dead Prez, Talib Kweli, Chamillionaire, Papoose, Tupac, Mos Def, Tonedeff, Kanye West, Immortal Technique, Dizzee Rascal, Lauryn

PREFACE

Hill, Substantial, Session, Wordsworth, Punchline, Canibus, Sage Francis, Cormega, Consequence, Outkast, Black Thought, Ludacris, Raekwon, the Coup, Masta Ace, and from various netcees from the Flocab Rhyme Boards and EmceeBattleForum.com. We apologize if you're favorite rapper didn't make this list. Obviously, there is no possible way to include every skilled emcee out there.

One of the best ways to improve as an emcee is by listening to great hip-hop and analyzing what the rappers are doing. All of the lyrics mentioned in this book are from songs that are worth buying. You can find a full list of albums and links to buy them on Flocabulary.com/artists.

Use this book to learn more about the various techniques that rappers use to craft amazing lines. But as with everything, don't just copy what's inside. When you spit, be sure to tap into your inner creativity and bring something real and personal. Those are the best rhymes: the ones that are not only technically interesting but also come from a deeper, realer place. Whether you know it or not, we're all capable of writing rhymes like that.

Enjoy the book and always spit fire.

- Emcee Escher and Alex Rappaport

PART ONE
FREESTYLING

Intro

Freestyle rapping (or freestyling or freeing) is improvising rap lyrics in real time. It's spitting lyrics off the top of your head. While some frontin' pseudo-freestylers actually just rap lyrics they wrote down and memorized, true freestylers make it up as they go.

Not every good freestyler drops a good album, but in general your freestyle skills are directly related to your overall rap skills. So when you start out rapping, start out freeing. Soon you'll be running ciphers like track meets.

> "I just try to think of what's important to the people in my surroundings and try to speak on it."
> – Wordsworth, on the key to freestyling

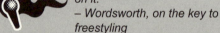

The Official Flocabulary 10-Pronged Technique for Learning to Freestyle

Step 1. Start Easy

No need to start off rhyming "the toasty cow's utter" with "most o' my flow's butter". No need to even rhyme. Just forget everything else and flow. The rhythm can be simple, the words might be 2nd grade level, but you're still freestyling as long as you make it up. This was my first freestyle rap, which I spit when I was 11 months old:

> *I am funny,*
> *I like bunnies,*
> *touch my tummy,*
> *mummy*

Step 2. Keep Flowing

You're going to make mistakes. You're going to sound stupid. Make your first freestyle rap verses your stupidest verses just to get them out of the way. Keep flowing. Can't think of a rhyme? Keep flowing! Stutter over words? Keep flowing. It's inevitable that at some point some of your lines won't rhyme, won't make sense, or that you will inadvertently diss yourself (I knew one guy who accidentally dissed himself all the time when we were freestyling), just keep flowing. If you make a mistake, do your best to incorporate your mistake into your next lines like this:

> *I drive you bananas, apples and oranges,*
> *ah.... damn, nothing rhymes with oranges,*
> *to make it rhyme, I squeeze it into orange juice,*
> *flow's tighter than small undies... yours are mad loose*

Another technique to use when you find yourself in a bind is to whip out a quick filler. Fillers are just little phrases that you can insert occasionally to give you more time to think of a dope line. Every emcee has his own fillers. For example, Eyedea says "I grab the microphone." Jin often says, "I'm (nasty) when I'm freeing." I usually say, "you know what I'm sayin'?"

Try to come up with a few fillers that you feel comfortable using. They'll bail you out of some awkward pauses. As you get better, try not to rely too heavily on your fillers.

Step 3. Rhyme in your mind ahead of time

Here's the biggest trick to freestyle rapping: as soon as you know what word you're going to end line 1 with, your mind should start racing to find out a word you can use at the end of line 2. Let's say your first line is, "I'm exhausted from doing summer reading." As soon as you realize that you're going to end the line with

Freestyle Guide 5

"reading", you should immediately think of something that rhymes, and might possibly be related:

> *meaning,*
> *weeding,*
> *beading,*
> *ceiling,*
> *teething*

Pick one and then try to carve the second line to lead toward that word. Let's say you pick "weeding", your next line might be:

> *I'm exhausted from doing summer reading,*
> *breaking my back digging holes, painting and weeding*

If you pick "meaning," you might say:

> *I'm exhausted from doing summer reading,*
> *my eyes skim the page but always miss the meaning*

The real trick of freestyling is to have your mind constantly racing ahead of what you're saying. This isn't easy, but you'll get quicker with practice.

Step 4. Write

Writing raps will help you freestyle. When you write, rhymes become imbedded in your head, and you're more likely to be able to pull these rhymes off the top of your head in a freestyle.

With that said, you should never spit a long pre-written verse at a cipher, but you can certainly use rhyming words and shorter phrases that you worked out before hand. When Eminem rhymes "Ewoks, treetops, and Reeboks" in a freestyle, you better believe he's thought of those rhymes before. He's still freeing, but he's using rhyme words he'd already worked out.

Sitting down and writing everyday will improve your freestyles. It will expand your memory of rhyming words, and it will give you experience working these words into clever lines. It's also a good idea to write a few multi-purpose bars that you can spit at a freestyle in case you get really stuck. Put those lines in a "Break Out Rhymes In Case of Emergency" box, and smash the glass when you need help. This isn't cheating; it's canny.

When you're writing these "in case of emergency" lines, make them strong and interesting, but not too ridiculously amazing. Don't do this:

I'm too good for school I can't sit in a chair, (free)
They pulling my leg, like they pulling my hair, (free)
Hit or miss, call it quits, rippin' hits a little bit too fast to figure it, (written)
But I'm sippin' it, too ridiculous the way I'm flippin' it, (written)

> *That's just the way that the rap goes,* (free)
> *Appealing to your eyeballs and your nose* (free)

You don't want you're "emergency" rhymes to be that obvious. Try to write rhymes that generally match your level of freestyle, but are clever and smart.

Step 5. Rap about things around you

This is definitely the best way to prove to the crowd that you're really freestyling and not just spitting something you wrote in your room the night before. It's also a huge crowd-pleaser, 'cause its impressive and it makes everyone real glad that they're hanging out with you. Rap about things you see. Incorporate objects, actions, people, clothing, situations, and sounds into your rap. When I'm in the shower, I'll rap about what kind of soap I'm using:

> *Trying hard to get clean, maybe just a smidgen,*
> *I use ghetto Dove soap, also known as pigeon*

Or at a battle competition, this is crucial. You've got to spit things specific about your opponent. These are the hardest-hitting punches. Take Eminem's freestyle (not really a freestyle - because it was pre-written to sound like a freestyle) on 8-mile. He's battling a guy named Lotto who's wearing a tight, white tank top:

> *Lookin' like a cyclone hit you,*

> *Tank top screamin', 'Lotto, I don't fit you!*

If you're rapping while driving around in your car, rap about how you feel or things you see.

> *I'm hungry driving in this old Volvo,*
> *I think I'll stop by Olive Garden and drink some olive oil*

Step 6. Include Metaphors

Metaphors and similes are an advanced but important part of freestyle rapping. They are often found in a rapper's funniest and cleverest lines, and they really differentiate beginners from skilled emcees. Take Talib Kweli's lines:

> *We're like shot clocks, interstate cops and blood clots,*
> *my point is... your flow gets stopped*

Metaphors and similes are really the backbone of an advanced rapper. He'll spit more comparisons than a door-to-door salesman to sink the competition like a leaky submarine. Learn how to use metaphors correctly, and your rhymes will not only be funnier and smarter, but they'll sound better too. Take Kanye's line:

> *Ooh, girl, your breath is harsh,*
> *cover your mouth up like you've got SARS*

Step 7. Reference current events

See what Kanye did in that line above? He snuck in the cultural reference. Other than amazing in-rhyming and dope metaphors, the most impressive thing a freestyle rapper can do is make timely references to culture and current events. Let's say, for example, that you are at a cipher, rapping with some of your friends (dissin' each other, just goofin' around), and the day before you remember reading that Oprah recently lost 200 pounds. How dope is it if you throw that in your rhymes:

> *You big now, but you 'bout to get cut down,*
> *smaller than Oprah Winfrey dropping 200 pounds*

I recently heard an emcee reference soaring gas prices:

> *Fast? son, that ain't fast.*
> *I'm rising faster than the price of gas*

The sooner you can reference it, the better.

Step 8. Pass the mic like it's contagious

Rap in ciphers - groups of two or more rappers playing off of reach other, trading verses. This is a great way to improve and it's hell of fun. One of your friends can beat box, you can throw a beat on the stereo, or just freestyle over nothing. Take turns, cutting in whenever you want or when someone "passes you the mic" (you probably won't have an actual mic). Never drop the invisible mic! Pick it up and pass it!

Work off of other people's rhymes. If they throw in something about the bible, pick up that theme and run with it. Try to stick to similar topics, or riff off of topics in creative ways. Expand / reference their lines. When my friends and I cipher, we like to kick it about random stuff that we all know about, like our personal lives.

Me:
> *Derek's life is tough, his job is rough,*
> *plus Suparna took all his dopest stuff,*
> *for her apartment in NYC,*
> *'cause that's where she be,*
> *holding down a job at a publishing company*

Derek:
> *Yeah, my life is tough, but not that hard,*
> *'cause I spend all my nights watching Sponge Bob,*
> *Escher you the one with the job that sucks,*
> *asking people if they want more pepper on their halibut*

Or take this example from Eminem's battle with Lotto from 8-Mile. Lotto starts off by referencing the old 50's TV show, *Leave it to Beaver*. Eminem picks it up and spits it right back, referencing all the characters from the show.

Lotto:
> *Fu** 'Lotto,' call me your leader*
> *I feel bad I gotta murder that dude from "Leave It To Beaver"*

Eminem:
> *Ward, I think you were a little hard on the Beaver*
> *So was Eddie Haskell, Wally, and Ms. Cleaver*

Step 9. When you're in a cipher, think ahead

One of the great things about rapping in ciphers is that after you spit one verse you get a break before you spit again. This break is your best friend. It's during this break that you'll be listening and responding to your friends' verses. But you'll also be planning out your next verse.

Whenever I'm in a cipher, I never like to get back on the mic until I've written 4-6 quality lines. To be most impressive, these lines will be about things around you, or they'll be about something your friend said in his verse. Let's say your friend is wearing a shirt that has Daffy Duck on it. While he's spitting, you can write a line like this:

> *I know you've had a tough year*
> *and had some crappy luck,*

> *but why you gotta wear a shirt*
> *with the face of Daffy Duck*

That's not an amazing line, but I guarantee you that in a cipher people will go nuts over that. (Make sure to point at his shirt as you say it). I always try to write 2-3 of those rhyming couplets before I spit again. Usually I'll drop one right away and then use the other two later in the verse.

Step 10. Listen and Practice

Freestyling, like sculpting or shooting three-pointers, takes an insane amount of practice. Practice as much as you can. Freestyle with homeless people, with your friends, and with your family. Listen to pro rappers who freestyle and try to analyze their styles. Rap all the time, practice all night and day. Practice might not make perfect, but it makes damn good!

Cipher Etiquette 101

> **droppin' knowledge**
> *"Everything I did, it made me tighter, and now I cipher with some of the best rhyme writers"*
> - Classified, Just the Way It Is

Rapping in ciphers (groups of people) is one of the most demanding tasks of the beginning emcee (after all, everyone's looking at you), but also the most fun. Spit in ciphers as much as you can, and be sure to follow these simple rules.

*Don't Give Excuses
I've heard some emcees say, "when you mess up, just cough a few times and people will think you've got a cold. They won't know you couldn't think of any rhymes." That's terrible advice. If you mess up, just ride it out. After a few times coughing, everyone is going to know that you're fronting anyway. Also: if you're freestyling over a beat or someone beat-boxing, don't blame your mistakes on the beat-box. Nobody likes a guy who blames everyone else for his own mistakes.

*Help Out Your Friends When They Mess Up
Truly one of the classiest things you can do in a cipher is to help out a fellow emcee when they slip up. Not

only does it help out the emcee who just messed it, it helps maintain the good vibe and flow of the cipher itself. When you sense that an emcee is running out of rhymes or can't think of anything (or if he starts "coughing"), take the rhyme over and finish it for him. You can then pass it right back, or you can keep rhyming.

*Don't Hog the Mic
The whole point of a cipher is to share rhymes, interact, and listen. If you want to rhyme 90% of the time then you can go rap in front of the mirror. Listen to other people, how many bars they're spitting, and try to do about the same. In certain ciphers, it's fine to interrupt someone to pick up on their lines, but don't go barging in all time or they're going to get pissed off.

*Pass it with Class
Depending on your cipher, emcees might be interrupting each other, they might be 'handing off the mic,' or both. Passing or handing off the mic means that you spit a bar or two about who's coming next. In a (mostly prewritten) freestyle with Canibus and Jurassic 5, Canibus goes, "now let me hand it to my man on the right, so he can spark the mic". That's a good pass. The other kind involves actually calling out the person's name, like the Sugarhill Gang does in "Rapper's Delight": "now next on the mic is my man Hank, now come on Hank sing that song".

CIPHER ETIQUETTE

*Listen and Respond
Just because you're trying to think of some ill rhymes while your friend is spitting doesn't mean you should ignore him or her. Listen to their verse and respond vocally when they spit something impressive. A good "ohhh!" or "damn!" works fine. Just don't leave your homey hanging.

*Invite Strangers into the Circle
Ciphering is a great way to meet new people and new emcees. If you're on a street corner, let people step in and see what they've got. I always like to invite random people into a cipher (old, young, boys, girls). To my mind, the more diversity the better.

Freestyle Rap Games

> **droppin' knowledge**
>
> *"When you first come in the game,
> they try to play you,
> then you drop a couple of hits,
> look how they wave to you"*
> - Jay-Z, Encore

This collection of easy-to-play games might not be as exciting as *Grand Theft Auto San Andreas*, but at least it won't make you think you can steal people's cars. All of them will improve your freestyle abilities, and with the right people they can be fun as hell.

The Circle of Rhymes

Rules:
This is as simple a game as they come. Gather in a circle with your friends. Someone starts by saying a word (i.e. "leather"). The next person has to think of a rhyme for that word in less than five seconds (i.e. "feather"). This continues around the circle until someone messes up (i.e. "leader"). The person who messes up steps out of the circle, and the game starts again. The last person standing wins.

Solo Variation:
Think of a word and try to come up with as many

FREESTYLE RAP GAMES

rhymes for it as you can in 1 minute. Then move on to another word and do the same. Play this game again a week later and do the same words. See if you can improve your score.

The Circle of Lines

Rules:
Similar to "The Circle of Rhymes," only this time each person has to actually spit a line that rhymes. The first person starts with a line ("The police are too racist in this town"). Then it passes to the right. The lines don't have to be the same length, or relate to each other ("I'm scared of clowns"), but you get more respect if they do relate (i.e. "the police beating brothers, handing out beat downs"). Each person has roughly five seconds to spit their line. Last person standing wins.

Solo Variation:
Spit as many lines as you can that all have the same rhyme.

Group Raps

Rules:
Similar to "The Circle of Lines," only not every single line has to rhyme. What you're doing is creating a rap verse. The first person spits one line on anything they want ("People don't give a damn about politics"). The second person has five seconds to respond with a rhyme that makes sense ("because politicians sell out

like they turning tricks"). Now the third person can spit anything they want as long as it's on topic. They don't have to rhyme ("the only time people vote is for American Idol"). The fourth person has to rhyme with that ("speak for yourself, I know you don't vote like I do"), etc... This game works best with an odd number of people. The person who messes up steps out, or you can play non-competitively.

Google "I'm Feeling Lucky" Freestyle Madness

Requirements:
High-speed internet access

Rules:
This is a favorite of mine. Get on your computer and put on a beat. (You can listen to one of the hip-hop instrumentals on Flocabulary.com, if you want). One person (the 'operator') gets on the computer and google searches for anything they want. They click the "I'm Feeling Lucky" button, so that a webpage immediately comes up. The other people have to freestyle about whatever is on that webpage. The operator can switch the page at anytime by searching for something else. The more random the searches are the better (try *stray dogs*, *lasagna*, *rollerskates*, *India*, etc...). You can also do this with image searches and freestyle about the images.

Freestyle Rap Games

Solo Variation:
Do this yourself. You're the operator and the rapper.

Other Variations:
You can easily play this kind of game without a computer. Just have one kid throw out random topics that you (and your friends) have to rhyme about. Or you can play this with the TV or radio on. Rhyme about whatever you see or hear.

PART TWO
ELEVATING YOUR RHYMES

Intro

In this section, we break it all down like a scientist mapping the human genome. Various lyrical techniques are tackled individually, crystallized into their component parts. You can read this section through all the way, or you can tackle individual sections separately. The suggested exercises are obviously optional, but will help you put the knowledge in these pages into your own rhymes.

This whole section is based on analyzing the techniques used by the best emcees in the history of music. Developing your own ability to analyze will not only help you learn from your own favorite rappers (who may or may not be mentioned in this book), it will also give you a tool for life. Before Lebron James takes the floor against an opponent, he's studied that opponent. He's read reports, he's watched hours of video, he and the coaching staff have broken down and analyzed the other team for weaknesses. You better believe that Lebron would be a worse basketball player if he didn't have that analytic ability.

Whatever you do professionally will tax your analytic skills too. People who are able to quickly study and quickly learn, are those that are most successful in every field. Emcees included.

Slant Rhyme

> **droppin' knowledge**
>
> *"This thing called rhyming is no different than coal mining, we both on assignment to unearth the diamond."*
> - Mos Def, Travellin Man

The basis of rap is rhyme, and an emcee is just a painter with rhyming words, a poet with flow. It might sound obvious to some, but one of the best ways you can excel as an emcee is by picking better rhyming words. It's all like Rakim says on "I Know You Got Soul":

> *I start to **think** and then I **sink**
> into the paper like I was **ink**,
> when I'm writing I'm trapped in between the <u>line</u>,
> I escape when I finish the <u>rhyme</u>*

Reread that. That right there is the dopest, most beautiful summary of what it is to be a rapper. You go into your own mind, sink into the paper, you're using words but they trap you like bars in a jail cell unless you conquer them with rhyme. It's rhyming that sets the emcee free and gives him control over his raps. It's rhyming that lets the emcee rock the microphone, and get a crowd jumping. It's rhyming that forms the foundation of your flow.

As Rakim demonstrated, however, we're not talking about "Hickory Dickory Dock." In rap, not every rhyme has to be at the end of a line. Rhymes don't have to be in a certain order or a certain word length. In fact, some of the most prevalent types of rhyme in hip-hop don't rhyme perfectly at all. They're called slant rhymes.

Slant Rhyme vs. Perfect Rhyme

Here are some definitions from the *American Heritage Dicitonary*:

> **Perfect Rhyme** (noun): Rhyme in which the final accented vowel and all succeeding consonants or syllables are identical, while the preceding consonants are different.

This is what most people think of when they think rhyme. Examples of perfect rhyme are: *cat, hat, bat; cake, bake, fake*. Perfectly rhyming words don't have to be spelled the same way; it's all about sound. For example: *great, late; height, fight; bought, knot*. Those are all perfect rhymes. And the words don't have to be the same length either. For example: *rider, beside her; dutiful, unbeautiful*. Those are all examples of perfect rhyme.

Perfect rhyme will work fine in a lot of situations. But hip-hop innovators (and poets before them) found it too limiting. Rappers began using slant rhyme to allow them more freedom to express themselves. Here is the definition of slant rhyme from the *AHD*:

> **Slant Rhyme** (noun): A partial or imperfect rhyme, often using assonance or consonance only. Also called half rhyme, near rhyme, oblique rhyme, and off rhyme.

You could think of slant rhymes as "almost rhymes." Examples are: *heat, heart; cow, no; dry, died; love, fluff*. Slant rhymes are words that sound somewhat similar, but don't really rhyme.

In the Rakim line quoted earlier, he rhymes the word "rhyme" with "line." Those words don't actually rhyme with each other. "Rhyme" rhymes with "time, dime, mime, I'm, and crime." "Line" rhymes with "mine, pine, whine, and tine." But the two words sound remarkably close. So Rakim uses slant rhyme to "finish the line."

When Slant Rhyme is a Must

When should you use slant rhyme? Anytime. But there are moments when using slant rhyme isn't an option; it's a must.

1. The word has no perfect rhyme

There are lots of words in English that don't have

perfect rhymes. Here are a few: *silver, purple, month, angst, sixth, breadth, ninth, pint, wolf, opus, monster, dangerous, marathon, napkin, hostage, discombobulate* and many, many more.

As you're writing raps, if you ever wanted to rhyme with any of those words you couldn't. Not unless you used slant rhyme. That's exactly what Nas does in "NY State of Mind." He uses the word "dangerous," which has no perfect rhyme, but he makes it flow anyway:

> *I got so many rhymes I don't think I'm too* **sane**,
> *Life is <u>parallel</u> to <u>Hell</u> but I must* **maintain**,
> *And be* **prosperous**, *though we live* **dangerous**,
> *Cops could just arrest me,* **blaming us**, *we're held like* **hostages**

He slants rhymes "prosperous, dangerous, blaming us," and "hostages," to get his point across. And his flow doesn't suffer for it.

You can find a list of slant rhymes for words with no perfect rhyme in *Appendix III* at the end of this book.

2. Avoid Tired Rhymes

The other time when slant rhyme is really crucial is when you're dealing with a rhyme that is really stale and played out. For example, how many times have you heard the word "knowledge" rhymed with

SLANT RHYME

"college." Damn! People overuse that rhyme like skeezy businessmen use too much cologne. In order to avoid that, all we need to do is use slant rhyme.

Knowledge – *mall kids, honest, ballas, taller, Paul Wall did, on it, admonish, cabbage.*

The great thing about slant rhyme is that it helps you avoid one of most dangerous pitfalls for beginning emcees: obvious rhymes. If a listener can tell what you're going to say before you say it, that's almost always a bad thing. It basically means that you're not being creative, you're just repeating tired rhymes. So use slant rhymes to avoid falling into that trap.

For example, instead of rhyming "money" with "funny" or "honey," try using slant rhyme: *gin rummy, Sunday, dummy, crumbly, Tony, blunt be, hunt me, some tea, plenty.*

Pro Example

> I see no changes
> wake up in the morning and I **ask myself**,
> is life worth living should I **blast myself**?
> I'm tired of bein' poor and even worse I'm black,
> my stomach hurts so I'm
> lookin' for a purse to snatch,
> cops give a damn about a <u>negro</u>,
> pull the trigger kill a ni**a he's a <u>hero</u>
>
> Tupac, "Changes"

Some artists use line after line of slant rhyme, but because of their flow and the way they pronounce the words, you don't even hear the words as being slant rhymes. Take a look at Tupac's verse on "Changes."

He slant rhymes "ask" with "blast," "black" with "snatch," and "negro" with "hero." It allows him more freedom to determine the content of what he's saying (he has more words to choose from), and it makes his lines innovative and creative.

Practice This
Write a few bars using some very obvious rhyme words ("cat, hat,"). Then go back and replace the rhyme words with slant rhymes and rewrite the verse. See how it changes your verse.

Rhyme Scheme

> **droppin' knowledge**
>
> "It is important to write in a way that has your song working on multiple levels. Not everybody can catch the nuances of alliteration, word play, multi-syllabic rhyme schemes, internal rhyme, etc… but if they catch one thing and they can make sense of it and enjoy it then [you] have succeeded."
> – Sage Francis

Rhyme Scheme

The rhyme scheme in a rap verse (or in a poem) is where the rhymes fall in relation to other words or lines. In a simple verse, the rhymes will fall only at the end of each line. In English class, when analyzing poetry, the rhyme scheme would be written out like this:

Rats in the front room, roaches in the back,	A
junkies in the alley with the baseball bat,	A
I tried to get away, but I couldn't get far,	B
cuz the man with the tow truck repossessed my car	B

These lines are from the 1982's "The Message" by Grandmaster Flash and the Furious Five. The flow is by the lead emcee, Melle Mel (who we'll discuss in more detail in the chapter on flow). These lines show off the most basic rhyme scheme possible. There are no internal rhymes and there is no multi-syllabic rhyming. All of the rhymes fall right on or near the second snare kick, the 4th beat of the bar, which musicians call *the four*.

Mapping the rhyme scheme out like that (AABB) works fine when the lyrics are simple, but not when the rapper's start dropping internal rhymes.

Rhyme Scheme Notation

The method used in this book is to highlight matching rhymes by formatting them the same way. So some rhyming words are bold, some italicized, some underlined, some bold-italicized, some underlined-bold, etc... Here's an example from Dead Prez's "Hell Yeah":

> *Better* plot *for the* **paper**,
> *we been living in the* dark *since* **April**,
> *on the* <u>candle</u> *gotta get a* <u>handle</u>,
> *my homie got a 25 autom**atic added** to the* <u>camper</u>
> *Ni**a* **get** *the phone* <u>book</u>
> <u>look</u> *up in the yellow* **page**,
> <u>**let**</u> *me* <u>**tell**</u> *you how we fin to get* **paid**

With a verse that complex, there's no way we can use the old ABAB rhyme scheme notation. Using our notation, you can easily see where the rhymes fall in the lines, and how often the rapper is using in-rhymes and multies. This will be the system we use throughout the book.

The very basic rhyme scheme from "The Message" is a fine place to start as you beginning writing raps and freestyling. By having only one rhyming word per line and placing it at the end of the line, it will free your mind up to craft some quality lines that make sense. When you're freestyling, it's always better to spit lines that make sense than to spit lines that sound good but don't mean anything.

As you progress as a writer and a freestyler, you're going to want to get away from simple rhymes and a simple scheme. In-rhymes and multies (discussed later) are great ways to introduce variation into your rhymes. But you can also mix up your rhymes just by altering the rhyme scheme. In the Dead Prez example above, the rapper Sticman varies his rhymes throughout, so that you never know when the next rhyme sound is going to come at you.

Think outside the box. Not every single line has to rhyme. Don't be afraid to break out of the standard "rhyme-word-on-4" mold.

In-Rhyme

droppin' knowledge

"The best thing I can do is pretty much out-rap the guy. And when I say out-rap the guy — say, if he uses ten syllables in a line, I'm going to use fifteen. If he uses fifteen, I'm going to use twenty, twenty-five. If he's rhyming two or three words within two bars, I'm going to rhyme four or five words in two bars. I'm going to out-skill you."
– Bun B on rapping as a guest artist on other people's albums

"In-rhyme" is short for "internal rhyme." An in-rhyme is any rhyme that occurs internally within a line. Using them is a sure-fire way to improve your rhymes. Like a subtle ingredient in a recipe, in-rhymes can add big punch without calling too much attention to themselves.

Adding In-Rhyme

In-rhymes are rhymes that fall within the line itself. These words don't have to rhyme with the word at the end of line. They can rhyme on their own, or with any word in any other line. Here's a sample lyric that does not contain in-rhyme:

In-Rhymes

> *Moving quick like a pack of wolves **hunting**,*
> *Telling all of these false haters to stop **frontin'***

Those are some pretty boring lines. There's nothing lyrically interesting about them at all. But I can easily change that. I can look for words to change that will create in-rhymes. Like this:

> *Moving **fast** like a **pack** of wolves **hunting**,*
> *Telling all of these <u>fake</u> <u>haters</u> to stop **frontin'***

By changing "quick" to "fast," I create an in-rhyme with "pack". Changing "false" to "fake," creates the rhyme with "hate". See how much better that sounds? Small changes make a big difference.

Start the Next Line with In-Rhyme

You can also use in-rhymes to rhyme with the words at the end of lines. For example, one common use is to start a line with a word that rhymes with the end of line before it. Like this from the Roots' "Next Movement":

> *yo the*
> *whole state of things in the world 'bout to **change***
> *black **rain** falling from the sky look **strange***

Black Thought uses the rhyme sound from the end of line one to start line two, and then uses it again at the end of line two. Plus, the way that Black Thought pronounces the words, "state" and "things" sound very similar to "change, rain, and strange."

Going Wilder

> **Pro Example**
>
> **Planted their feet** to build a **land of deceit**, plot*ted*, con*quered* and *spread* **disease** across *the* **seas**,
> it's the **Spanish fleet**,
> wel*come* to <u>America</u>, the <u>era</u> of early <u>terror</u> where Col*um*bus named the coun*try* out of <u>error</u>
>
> Akir, "I Want America"

But you can obviously go much wilder than that. Take a few lines from the rapper Akir. Akir is gifted underground emcee doing his thing in NYC. Already named the Source's "Next To Blow," he brings a unique flow that mixes smooth delivery, intelligent lyrics and lots of in-rhymes. I had the privilege of working with him on a Flocabulary track for the *Hip-Hop U.S. History* album, which teaches American history through rap music.

Akir came into our Times Square studio and I gave him a list of facts to incorporate into the rhyme. We put on a beat, and within minutes he had some sick rhymes to lay down. The method he used was to listen very

In-Rhymes

closely to the beat and find a flow that worked with it. As he spit, he'd put certain rhyme words right on certain drum fills and other sounds, to add a natural complexity to his verse. Plus he uses slant rhyme, in-rhyme, and mutlis together. Amazingly, he's also able to stay right on topic, discussing Columbus' arrival in America with ease.

Practice This
Rewrite a few bars you've already written, replacing words to create in-rhymes. Try not to sacrifice the meaning of what you wrote just to fit in rhymes.

Multies

Why take just vitamin C when you can get vitamin C and D in one pill? The creation of multi-vitamins launched a worldwide craze for multies, but what most of the world didn't realize is that rappers from Chuck D to Bun B were already serving up mulies in their raps.

Once a rare treat, multies are now being used in hip-hop more and more frequently as lyricists constantly try to outdo each other. Multies aren't necessarily harder to write than normal rhymes. They just take extra effort. You'll find that the effort is well worth it. Spit multies, and get your vitamin C.

droppin' knowledge

"The hardest thing for me to do, as far as writing a rhyme, is figuring out how it's going to go. Once I get in my mind that it's going to go 'da da da dadada da da,' then it's kind of like filling in the blanks. I take the typical words, or I pick a two-word, three-word pattern.

One of the things I'm known for is I was one of the first rappers to end their bars rhyming multisyllabically. The other day I put Curb Your Enthusiasm in a rhyme.

'Tell your homeboy to curb his enthusiasm / before I point my motherfu**in' Uzi at him'."
- Bun B

Part I - The Basic Lesson

What are multies?

Multi is short for "multi-syllable rhyme." Multies are phrases in which more than one syllable rhymes. Multies can be double, triple, quadruple (etc...) rhymes.

> Normal rhyme: *cat / hat*
> Multi rhyme: *my cat / hi-hat*
> Or a *longer* multi: *bit my cat / hit the hi-hat*

Southern rapper Ludacris loves featuring multies in his verses. Luda has a trademark delivery, in which he slows down and emphasizes the end of each line. This delivery works well when he slips in some clever multies.

> **Pro Example**
> *I'm never going nowhere, so don't **try me**, my music sticks in fans' veins like an **I.V.***
> **Ludacris, "Number One Spot"**

In the example from the track *Number One Spot*, Luadacris creates a multi with "try me" and "I.V." He could have just rhymed "me" with "V.", but by rhyming with the additional syllables (*try* with *I*) it becomes a multi.

What's the difference between multies and in-rhymes?

In-rhymes:
>*Don't be **silly** cover your **milli** I'm like **Billy***
>*Don't be **dumb** cover your **gun** I ain't **fun***
>   - Dizee Rascal, "Stand Up Tall"

Multies:
>*Punchlines that kill… my **hits'll bury ya**,*
>*I rap to myself on the bus like… **schizophrenia***

Why should I use multies?

Multies are hallmarks of all the dopest flows, and all the best rappers use them. They are more complex and more impressive than normal rhymes and so command a lot more respect. Multies add variation to your verse and will help you craft better rhymes.

How do I write multies?

Multies aren't that much harder to write than typical rhymes, they just take more time. Step one is to find a line that you want to start with. Take this line for example:

>*The elite force like army rangers and navy seals,*

Now we're going to create a ***multi*** with "navy seals." The first thing you want to do is list all the words that rhyme with "navy". The easiest way to do this is by using a rhyme dictionary (rhymezone.com) and listing the results, but keep in mind that this will only give you the 'perfect' rhymes, not the slant rhymes. Slant rhymes are very important, because they allow you to write more creative lines. This is especially true when you're writing multies, 'cause otherwise your lines might come out contrived and stupid. The other problem with rhyming dictionaries is that they do the work for you. If you take the time to actually think for yourself of all the rhymes for the word, you're more likely to get those rhymes in your head for future freestyles. I don't recommend rhyme dictionaries unless you're really stuck.

Perfect rhymes for **navy**:

> *gravy*
> *wavy*

Slant rhymes for **navy**:

> *maybe*
> *baby*
> *lady*
> *rabies*
> *weighty*
> *etc…*

Then repeat this process for the second word, in this case, "seals."

Perfect rhymes with ***seals***:

>deals
>eels
>feels
>heels
>meals
>peels
>reels
>squeals
>steals
>wheels

Slant rhymes for ***seals***:

>stales
>whales
>beans
>etc...

Now we go through the process of linking up *navy*-rhymes with *seals*-rhymes. There are lots of combinations, so try to pick some that make some sense:

>*Baby meals*
>*Wavy eels*
>*Lady squeals*
>*Gravy feels*
>*Weighty whales*

Then we pick one and write a line that makes sense:

MULTIES

> *I kick it operatic 'til that fat lady squeals*

or

> *your lyrics are stuffing,*
> *so now I know how gravy feels*

or

> *I'll call you Gerber*
> *cuz ya spittin' up some baby meals*

Write a bunch of them, and then pick the one that you like best to use. Or use a bunch of them in a row like this:

> *The elite force like army rangers and navy seals,*
> *I kick it operatic 'til that fat lady squeals*
> *your lyrics are stuffing, now I know how gravy feels,*
> *I'll call you Gerber*
> *cuz ya spittin' up some baby meals*

That's the simplest way to write multies. If you master that simple technique, you should already notice your lyrical skills improving.

Practice This
Take a common phrase or celebrity name (i.e. "train station" or "George Bush") and write out some multi-syllable rhymes using this method. Work the rhymes into some lines that make sense together.

Part II - The Advanced Lesson

Ok, so you've worked through the basic lesson and you want to take it further. The next thing we need to cover is the difference between prominent (or "stressed") syllables and silent (or "unstressed") syllables. It's the same thing that your English teacher was teaching you when you did that Shakespeare lesson on iambic pentameter. In this case, we're going to use it to figure out how to create long strings of quality multies that flow well. The general rule is this: you have to rhyme with the prominent syllables; you can ignore the silent ones.

Prominent vs. Silent

The basic idea is that when you speak or rap there are certain syllables that you stress or put emphasis on and certain syllables that you don't. When analyzing poetry, you'd place an accent mark (/) over the prominent syllables and a dash (-) over the silent syllables.

For example, say this out loud:

Today is the first day of the rest of my life

The meter (a map of which syllables are stressed and which are not) would be something like this:

```
   -  /  - -  /   /  - -  /   - -  /
```
Today is the first day of the rest of my life.

This is a typical example because often times "little" words (to, is, the, of) are silent. Obviously, when we're talking about a silent syllable, we don't mean literally silent. Silent just means it's not prominent.

The simplest way of figuring out which syllables are prominent and which are silent is just to say the line out loud and listen to what you pronounce strongly and what you don't.

Why Did I just Learn that?

Because with multies it's important to make sure you're rhyming with all the prominent syllables. But you don't have to rhyme with the silent syllables.

For example, take this line:

Behind my house is the most twisted of trees

If I want to write a multi rhyme with "twisted of trees," the first thing I need to do is figure out what is prominent and what isn't. So I'll map it out like this:

```
   -  /  -  /   - -  /    /  - -  /
```
Behind my house is the most twisted of trees

All I really have to pay attention to is the rhyming phrase, "twisted of trees." As you can see, the prominent sounds are "twist" and "trees." The silent sounds are "ed" and "of". That means that when I'm writing my multi, I need to rhyme with "twist" and "trees", but I don't need to rhyme with the "ed" or the "of".

So these work:

Mystical knee
Listen to me
Mess with the bees

Then I just pick one and write a line to it:

Behind my house is the most twisted of trees,
I always ignore the birds, but I mess with the bees

Even though "ed of" doesn't rhyme with "with the", it doesn't matter because they're unstressed syllables. The line still flows. Take another example from Eminem's verse on D12's "My Band". He uses the line:

/   -   /
*I just think you're trying to steal the **light** from **me***

In that line "light" and "me" are accented, but "from" isn't. So he doesn't worry about rhyming with "from," just the other words. Like this:

*I just think you're trying to steal the **light** from **me**,*
*Yesterday Kuniver tried to pull a **knife** on **me**,*
*'Cuz I told him Jessica Alba's my **wife** to **be***

What About Longer Multies?

I'm glad you asked. Some rappers (especially underground rappers) like to string together long as hell multies to impress their listeners. You don't always have to do this, but if you can drop a long-string multi occasionally, it will hit like a sound bomb.

Take this line:

/   -   /   /
Always on point with words that cut sharp

If we rhymed with "sharp" it would not be a multi. If we rhymed with "cut sharp" it *would* be a multi. Instead of just that, let's try rhyming with "words (that) cut sharp" to make a long multi. Remember, because "that" isn't prominent, we can ignore it. We just need to rhyme with *words*, *cut*, and *sharp*. I'm going to use a lot of slant rhymes in order to make a line that makes sense. Using the process of rhyme generating described before we get:

nerds that aren't smart
burns the white tarp
swords that touch heart

> *worms make bad art*
> *nervous you might fart*

Then we put them together:

> *Always on point with **words that cut sharp**,*
> *I'm a paradox like **nerds that aren't smart***

Or we can rewrite a little, and include another multi in there as well. Remember, it's always a good idea to revisit lines and rework them. Cut out the weak stuff, and add more quality stuff.

> *I spit **swords that touch hearts** and **words that cut sharp**,*
> *You're living proof that some **nerds are not smart***

> **Practice This**
> Write some 3 or 4 syllable multies, and then add them into your lines. Try to put more than one multi per line (as Papoose and Eminem do in the following section).

Who is the King of Multies?

Without a doubt, one rapper uses multies more than any other, and that rapper is Eminem. In fact a lot of his sick flow comes from his creative use of multi rhymes. You'll find multies in all of his songs. The ones below are just particularly strong examples. Take these bars from "The Real Slim Shady":

> But Slim *what if you* win *wouldn't **it be weird**?*
> *Why* so you *guys* could just *lie* to *get me here*,
> So you could *sit me here* next to ***Britney Spears***
> I think Christina Aguilera better ***switch me chairs***
>
> — Eminem, "The Real Slim Shady"

Here's what's so dope and amazing about those "Real Slim Shady" lines. Eminem doesn't just rhyme with the prominent syllables, he rhymes with the silent one too ("be, me, ney" are unstressed). He also uses a lot of multies with the same rhyme pattern: 5 in 4 lines.

How did he do that? He probably wanted to write a rhyme making fun of Britney Spears, so he started with her name and started generating multies off of it. He could have used others, but he found some that matched what he was trying to say. The lesson: always start with the word or phrase that is most important.

> *His* **palms** *are sweaty*, knees weak, **arms** *are heavy*
> There's **vomit on his** *sweater **already***, **mom's spaghetti**
> He's *nervous*, but on the *surface* he looks **calm and ready**
> To drop bombs, *but he* keeps **on forgetting**
>
> — Eminem, "Lose Yourself"

Those "Lose Yourself" rhymes are some of Eminem's absolute best, and that's saying a lot. What he does here lyrically is all out amazing. He uses lots of multi-rhymes and in-rhymes, not seperately but together to weave a complex lyrical web.

He uses 5-6 multies in just four lines, but he also repeats the "palms" sound in other words. It's echoed in "drop" and "bombs," but also in "vomit" and "on his," which is itself a little multi. The killer for me is the use of "keeps" in the last line, which rhymes with "knees weak" in the first. Study those lines, because they're as complex rhyme-wise as some analytic calculus.

How Many Multies Should I Use?

That's up to you. Some rappers use multies only occasionally, while others (like Eminem) rhyme almost exclusively with multies. Try not to let multies control your rhymes. The great thing about Eminem's verse on "Lose Yourself" is that he never sacrifices the meaning to squeeze in a multi.

On the next page is a unique example of a verse that rhymes over and over again with the same multi-syllable sound. The lyrics are from Papoose's track "Thug Connection." An underground rapper from NYC, Papoose is making a name for himself by demonstrating not only his lyrical powers, but also his versatility. He's been featured on tracks with Busta

Rhymes and even Shaquille O'Neil. This verse is a string of 30 different multies that all have the same (or similar) rhyme. Some people would definitely find this kind of rhyming excessive, but to others it's a jaw-dropping lyrical achievement.

Pro Example

My **lyrical tendency's** equivalent to a **critical felony**
Precise behind bars like a **criminal's penalty**
Pinnacle definitely, hold so much jewels in my **miracle memory**
It's like I'm a **physical treasury**
Deep into weaponry, psychotic ni**as **who envy me**
Wanna be nuts, so I bust nuts like my **genitals sexually**
Punished in my mother's stomach by **swimmin through Hennessy**
I was born with a **difficult destiny**, not your **typical mentally**
Givin my **vision through treacheries**
Syllable therapy, invincible **visual energy**
No **artist identity resemble me**, I flow like a **mineral chemically**
Cause I flow with a **chemical chemistry**
I can flow like the **river through Tennessee**
The **mystical seventh sea**, or currency at the **Senegal embassy**
At birth although it's **umbilical regularly**
They cut a mic chord and **disconnected me**
Leaders **political threaten me** for what I write in my **lyrical melody**
While others broke laws, I broke **lyrical legacies**
Flip forever, **live for infinity, respect the P**
It's Papoose, I conquered this **caliber, next degree**

Papoose, "Thug Connection"

Wordplay

Wordplay has been used by everybody from Shakespeare to Atmosphere to make audiences *ooh* and *ahh*. The best rappers combine wordplay and metaphors to create amazing lines that people remember and tell their grandkids about.

> **Pro Example**
> What you get on, it's fam you can't trust,
> Words and Punch
> **make rappers March like the third month**
> Punchline, "Twice Inna Lifetime"

What is Wordplay?

An instance of wordplay in rap is when words signify two or more different things that make sense in the context of the line. Wordplay is literally just playing with the meanings of words.

This is made possible by the fact that words in the English language (and most languages) can have multiple meanings. Words can have multiple dictionary definitions, scientific definitions, colloquial definitions and slang definitions. The skilled rapper can bounce between these meanings to create a line that knocks a crowd off their feet. This is another way in which having a big vocabulary is a real benefit to your rhyme-writing.

In the example that opened this chapter, Punchline plays on the two definitions of the word "march" (meaning 'to walk') and "March" ('the month after February'). In doing so, he creates a line that stops you in your tracks, because it's so damn clever. You'll notice that most instances of wordplay in rap involve metaphors as well. Here's another example from the same song. This is Wordsworth playing with the meaning of "stereotype":

> *Revive or ruin, my theories of mics,*
> *Sony or Aiwa, black or white, I fit in all stereotypes*

Creating Wordplay

How are you supposed to write lines like that? Follow these steps and don't do too many drugs.

Step 1. Pay Attention to New Words

Pay attention to words and their meanings in your life. When you read or hear words that you don't know, write them down and then look up their definition.

Step 2. Look for Multiple Definitions

When you do look up a word, don't just read the first definition in the dictionary, read all the definitions. This is crucial because wordplay is based on messing around with multiple definitions.

Step 3. Think About Words You Already Know

Do this exercise: look around you wherever you are and make a list of the things you see. You could write it down, or do it in your head. Now go through each object and try to think if there are alternate meanings for that word. If there are, take note of them.

For example, say I'm on the bus. This is my list, with possible wordplay listed after each one:

> **Bus** – a bus is a big vehicle for moving people. It's also the nickname of Jerome Bettis, the former running back for the Pittsburgh Steelers. A busboy busses tables; he clears them. Bus' (short for bust) can mean a lot of things: bust off, shoot, rhyme, break out.
>
> **Driver** – a driver is a person who is steering a car or bus. A driver is also the club you use in golf to hit the ball off the tee. Driver also sound like "drive her."
>
> **Seat** – a place where you sit. [Now I couldn't think of any for 'seat,' so I went to the dictionary, and this is what I got:] A seat can be your "buttocks" (that's what the dictionary says). A seat can also be a position on a board of trustees or committee. A member of congress also runs for a seat.

I could keep going, but I'll stop there. In general, the more you train yourself to think this way, the more easily these double-meanings will come to you.

Step 4. Create a Line Using Double-Meanings

Take a double meaning that you've observed and try to craft some lines out of it. Here's what I can do with the three above. These lines don't rhyme together, they would be used apart:

> *I'm a driver like what Tiger Woods holding,*
>
> *I used to be a busboy like Jerome Bettis' son,*
>
> *Missed the bus, like a senator I'm running for a seat.*

None of those are the kind of wordplay that would make you stop in your tracks. If I was writing a song I probably wouldn't use any of those. But I did that with three random words. As with everything, you're going to create a lot of bad, unusable lines before you find the rhymes you like.

Step 5. Study Slang

You can also start with a slang word and look at the different meanings. A lot of slang terms have dictionary definitions along with their street definitions:

Word – slang def / dictionary def

Ice – diamonds / frozen water
Cheddar – money / cheese
Sick – good / physically ill
Dope – good / somebody stupid / drugs

Then take these and write lines playing on the different meanings:

I've got more cheddar than a Wisconsin farmer

Rhymes sicker than lyme disease and gangrene
  - Pharoah Monch, "Right Here"

I'm diarrhea ni**a, you ain't ready for this sh**
  - Little Brother, "Flash and Flare"

Step 6. Use Idioms

You can also create wordplay by studying idioms. Idioms are phrases in a language that have a meaning other than what they say literally. For example, "piece of cake" means both literally a piece of cake and something that's easy. Idioms are a great place to start for wordplay because they inherently have double meaning. The rapper Legacy from Little Brother uses the idiom "hold my own" (meaning to be as strong as anyone else on a team) and raps: "***I hold my own like masturbation.***" Get the idea?

Flip to the back of the book to *Appendix I – Idioms* for a long list of idioms that you can use to create wordplay.

Step 7. Put It All Together

Then just put it all together to write some lines:

> This is **off the top** like the foamy head on your beer,
> my metaphors are **over your head** like your wack ass hair,
> **stand clear** like Casper the ghost waiting in line,
> like Geoffrey Rush or shoe polish, dawg, I'm ready to **Shine**

In the above lines, I play with the meanings of words in each line, creating four different metaphors with wordplay. Here's another example from the underground rapper Session, on Tonedeff's "Quotables." He plays with the double meanings of "bug" and "spotted." You can usually count on the best underground rappers to drop some high quality wordplay and metaphors, and Session is no exception.

> **Pro Example**
> Puff an L and bug, cause I won't be swatted
> I can't be seen -
> I'll be a Dalmatian and still won't be spotted
> — Session, "Quotables"

> **Practice This**
> Use the idiom list in Appendix I to create some wordplay. Your line should play with the idiomatic definition of the phrase and its literal definition. Then write some rhymes that feature your wordplay.

On the Net

A lot of netcees on the Flocab Rhyme Boards like to write out their lines by capitalizing their wordplay, italicizing it or adding weird symbols. Like this netcee:

> *You should put Lipstick~On~Your~Head*
> *and Make~Up~Your~Mind*

Whether you want to do this is obviously up to you. On the plus side it alerts everyone to your wordplay. On the down side, it can make it harder to read the line straight through.

Metaphors

Time for metaphors: one of the most important elements for all the best rappers. Metaphors are also one of the most basic things you can use to elevate your rhymes. There are whole rappers (Punchline, Wordsworth, and others) who made a name for themselves almost exclusively on the strength of their metaphors. In other words, pay attention to this one.

> ### droppin' knowledge
>
> "People are tired of only hearing the tough talk with no meaning, of hearing that you're a drug dealer unless you explain some other dimension of it. So what you got guns? You sold drugs, who hasn't? You did time? Me and few million other people have too… Make it creative or get a therapist.
>
> It's not that rappers are too 'street' or 'too raw' for the audience, they just aren't talented—weak metaphors, similes that a four-year-old could come up with. I always hear "he got a hot flow." 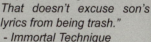 That doesn't excuse son's lyrics from being trash."
> - Immortal Technique

What is a metaphor?

Here's how the *American Heritage Dictionary* defines it:

Metaphor (noun) - A figure of speech in which a word or phrase that ordinarily designates one thing is used to designate another, thus making an implicit comparison, as in *"a sea of troubles"* or "All the world's a stage" (Shakespeare).

That's a good definition. In hip-hop, that definition gets even broader. A metaphor is basically a creative comparison between two things. For example: "I'm going up faster than the price of gas" is considered a metaphor. "The price of chicken is going up faster than the price of beef" is not a metaphor (because it isn't creative; it's obvious). Take a look at these much more impressive examples.

Pro Examples

Like Slick Rick the Ruler
I'm cooler than a ice brick,
got soul like those afro picks, with the black fist,
and leave a crowd dripping like John the Baptist
  - Black Thought on "Mellow My Man"

Me without a mic is like a beat without a snare...
I'm sweet like licorice, dangerous like syphilis
  - Lauryn Hill on "How Many Mics"

My rhymes are like shot clocks,
interstate cops and blood clots,
my point is... your flow gets stopped
  -Talib Kweli on "Hater Players"

Aren't Those Really Similes?

Some people differentiate between similes and metaphors. You're English teacher probably told you that a simile is a comparison that uses the word "like" or "as" and a metaphor is a comparison that doesn't. So those pro examples are actually similes? Well, technically they are. But we're going to use the term 'metaphor' to mean a larger category that includes metaphors, similies and other creative comparisons. Not only are they very similar techniques, but the way that you write them is almost exactly the same. Like Common says on that one song "1-9-9-9":

> *Hold the mic like a memory*
> *Ni**as say I'm nice with metaphors*
> *but these are similes*

Common's right. They are similes. But like most people in the rap world, we're going to call them metaphors to keep it simple.

Two Kinds of Metaphors

We're going to divide metaphors in two categories and tackle each one separately. First there are simple metaphors. And then there are metaphors that involve wordplay. The latter are much more impressive. In fact the most impressive lines in the history of hip-hop belong to rappers who created metaphors with wordplay. But let's start with the basics.

Simple Metaphors

First things first: you want to create a metaphor, you've got to have something to say. You can't make a metaphor out of thin air. So first think of the basic idea that you want to get across: what's the simplest thing you want to say? It could be almost anything:

> *I spit rhymes*
> *He's not smart*
> *She looks fly*
> *We're hungry*

All of these work, but we'll take just one for an example. Let's say we start with "I spit rhymes." Now think of some other things in the world that spit rhymes. It could be really simple:

> *A rapper at a show*
> *A slam poet*
> *A nursery rhyme*
> *A limerick*

Now we just put the first together with something from the second. We get:

I spit rhymes like a rapper at a show

That's a metaphor, but it's a pretty bad metaphor. It's simple and boring. The next step is to make it more

METAPHORS

specific and interesting. Think of a specific example of the "rapper at a show." For example:

> *Big Boi at Stankonia* (the name of his studio)
> *Jay-Z at the Garden* (Madison Square Garden)
> *T.I. at the Apollo*

Let's take the last one:

> *I spit rhymes like T.I. at the Apollo*

That's a much more solid line. It's not "oh damn, that was amazing," but it's solid. It's a good, simple metaphor.

Another Example:

We could complete the rhyme without using another metaphor. But why not put in one more just to keep the crowd on their feet? To complete the rhyme and write the next line, we'll work backwards. We'll think of all the words that rhyme with "Apollo":

> *Follow*
> *Hollow*
> *Swallow*
> *Wallow*
> *Kahlo* *

*Freda Kahlo was a painter

I'm going to use Kahlo, because it's very specific, so we can make a dope line with an unlikely reference that will catch people off guard. Now Freda Kahlo was a famous Mexican painter who was a lesbian. So I can play around with those facts:

> *I paint a picture of a Mexican like Freda Kahlo,*

or

> *I like kissing women like... Freda Kahlo*

Both of those are metaphors and they work, but I want something even better. So I go online and look up Freda Kahlo and I find this picture:

And I remember that Freda Kahlo had a huge unibrow (her eyebrows were connected in the middle of her face), so I can play off that fact.

METAPHORS

You've got a bigger unibrow than Freda Kahlo

I'm going to choose that one because it's smart, clever and I've never heard a rapper reference a unibrow before, so I know it's going to make the crowd go wild. Now we put them together:

I spit rhymes like T.I. at the Apollo,
you've got a bigger unibrow than… Freda Kahlo

There's no wordplay there, but it's some solid use of metaphors. I can file that rhyme away in the back of my mind in case I ever have to battle someone with a unibrow.

Pro Examples

My style of rhyming is ancient like Aztecs and Mayans, because I recognize it's all about timing
—Canibus, "100 Bars"

Cause, hey I stay flagrant with lyrics nastier than Tammy Faye bathing,
keep comp shook like charter planes when it's raining
—Tonedeff, "Heavyweights"

I take one of your chicks straight from under your armpit,
the black Brad Pitt, I mack 'til six in the AM
—Jay-Z, Punjabi MC "Beware of the Boys"

In all three of the pro examples, the rappers combine metaphors with other things: in-rhyme, multies and some nasty flow. But the metaphors on their own are strong.

Canibus goes way old school with a dope reference to Aztecs and Mayans, but also explains what he means by 'ancient': he is keeping it simple like the old school rappers, 'cause it's all about timing.

Tonedeff, a sick underground emcee who spits as fast as Twista, puts two metaphors in his bar, one after the other. The word 'comp' is just short for 'competition.'

Jay-Z's metaphor is the simplest (he's the "black Brad Pitt"), but that keeps with his easy-going style where nothing is over-written. In one sense, his metaphor might be the strongest because the image of Brad Pitt as a black man stops every listener in his tracks.

Metaphors with Wordplay

You know those lines that make your jaw drop? Those lines that are so smart you've got to rewind the track and listen to them again just to understand the intricacies? Most of those lines feature metaphors that involve wordplay. It's kind of like the one-two punch of a gifted lyricist, guaranteed to make the crowd scream. This technique creates some of the most amazing and memorable lines in hip-hop.

METAPHORS 65

Here's Kanye West on "Back Like That Remix":

> *We hit the spot to chill where the food get grilled*
> ***She order the Kobe beef like Shaquille O'Neal***

Kanye plays not only with the definition of beef (the meat from a cow and a feud between people) but also of the word Kobe (Kobe beef is especially tender beef from Kobe, Japan, while Kobe Bryant is the famous Lakers player who didn't get along with Shaq when Shaq was with the Lakers). In doing so, Kanye creates a metaphor with wordplay and a unique line.

How to Write Metaphors with Wordplay

The trick to creating these lines is really just to combine what you learned from the lesson on metaphors with what you learned from the lesson on wordplay. Start out with a simple statement. We can make it easy by choosing a phrase from the list of idioms (see *Appendix I*). For example:

> *I'll flip you the bird*

The expression "flip the bird" means sticking up your middle finger at someone. Now in order to create wordplay we just have to focus on the literal meaning of 'flipping birds'. So now we brainstorm a list of things that also 'flip birds':

> *Someone cooking chicken on a barbeque*
> *Someone wrestling pigeons*
> *A seagull who's an acrobat*

Now I just choose one and slip it after my original statement, adding the word "like" in between. I'll rework it a little to fit the flow and make it tigher. I can even use two of them in a row like this:

> *I'll flip you the bird like I'm barbequing chicken,*
> *Or like Hulk Hogan wrestling pigeons, so quit snitchin'*

That's all there is to it.

> **Pro Example**
>
> Lyrically deep like the teachings of Confucius
> spit ridiculous sh**, like a nipple-less tit -
> you're useless
> but **hang around** anyway hoping to **get felt**
> lyrically acidic when I spit it, making mics melt
> I should change my name to **Phillip**
> **'cause I'm screwing you up**
>
> Substantial, "Quotables"

This example from Substantial on the track "Quotables" is full of metaphors and metaphors with wordplay. In these lines, he deftly plays with the meaning of the words "hang," "felt," and "screw," which all have more than one meaning. He also puts in simple metaphors to add to the overall complexity of the lines.

METAPHORS

Practice This

Create some metaphors with and without wordplay. Which are your favorites? Analyze why some of them are stronger than others. Combine your favorites in a dope verse.

Vocabulary

> **droppin' knowledge**
>
> "It all started from writing. Like, when I was in school, I was real big in my English class, just with vocabulary, you know what I'm saying? I was never really lazy in English. I loved that class. I was never really lazy when it came to English. Everything else I hated, you know what I mean?"
> - Skillz

If a lyricist is a painter, then vocabulary is his paint. Without words, a rapper is no different than a mime: all he's got left are his hand gestures. Everyone has two vocabularies: a bank of words that they feel comfortable using, and a bank of words that they know the meanings of, but can't necessarily use.

As an emcee, it's your job to get your vocabulary of words you feel comfortable using to be as big as possible. Scientists say that in America the average adult vocabulary is between 10,000 – 20,000 words. The way some rapper's spit, I swear they're only using 500. Having a big vocabulary will allow you to write on topic more easily, and will make it easier to write metaphors, wordplay, in-rhymes and multies. And that's not just for the so-called 'conscious' rappers out there. That's true for battle rappers (definitively), and it's true for all the big ballas. It's like Bun B says on "Big Pimpin'":

*Pick up a book, you illiterate son of a b*tch,
and step up your vocab!*

How Do I Improve My Vocabulary?

There are lots of ways to improve your vocabulary. Reading is crucial. The more you read, the more you come in contact with new vocabulary words being used in context. When you come across a vocabulary word, either write it down or look it up straight away. If you're by a computer, using an online dictionary (like Dictionary.com) is a very fast way to find the meaning. I've also known emcees who carry pocket dictionaries with them everywhere they go, so whenever they come across a word, they're ready to learn it.

As this is the vocab section of the book and we are Flocabulary, we'd be remiss if we didn't mention our own product. We got some emcees together and created a hip-hop album that defines 500 SAT vocabulary words on 12 tracks. The idea for that came to me in high school: I realized that I could easily memorize the lyrics to dozens and dozens of rap songs, but I struggled to remember what the word "obstinate" meant. So we created Flocabulary and came out with our first CD+Book called *Flocabulary: The Hip-Hop Approach to SAT-Level Vocabulary Building*. You can get it on Flocabulary.com or in your local bookstore.

We think it's the best way to learn vocabulary words, since all of the words are defined in the tracks themselves. Memorize one song, and you've memorized the meaning of 50 words.

> **Pro Example**
>
> *Pop, crackle, snap like an elastic,*
> *I rock raps **ebulliently**, enthusiastically,*
> *I spit words with eagerness and **alacrity**,*
> *sip on my rhymes like a virgin daiquiri,*
> *I'm glad to be me, I'm **elated**, **exultant**,*
> *the **sovereign** of the land,*
> *I rule it like the sultan*
>
> Emcee Escher, "Pop, Crackle and Snap"

How Do I Use Vocabulary in My Rhymes?

More important than just spitting truly enormous words is spitting the correct word to fit your flow. Having a big vocabulary will allow you to find that correct word more easily. Here are a few tips on what to do and what to avoid.

Spit Big Words Sometimes

While you don't want to sound like you're randomly quoting a dictionary, dropping an occasional big word will add a lot to your verse. Take this example from Andre (3000) on "Wheelz of Steel":

> *We don't sell dope that you distribute,*
> *we don't contribute to your **clandestine** activity,*
> *my **soliloquy** may be hard for some to swallow*

That's good use of vocabulary. The words make sense in the context of the lyrics ("clandestine" means sneaky or shady, "soliloquy" is a speech given by one person, usually in a play). The use of "soliloquy" adds in-rhyme with "activity." And the use of "clandestine" adds some alliteration with "contribute," and "soliloquy" adds alliteration with "some" and "swallow." Overall, he's used two big words in a way that makes a lot of sense and definitively adds quality to his verse.

If You Don't Know it, Don't Drop it

Just because you think you know a big word, doesn't mean you should use it randomly. A big problem for some beginner emcees is that they try to front like their vocabulary is bigger than it really is by using huge words that they don't really understand. Don't use a big word that makes no sense just because it rhymes, like this:

> *I'd like to live on the moon, fly in space ships,*
> *always be by myself like it's **loquacious***

The word loquacious means talkative or chatty, so that rhyme makes no sense. It's an interesting slant rhyme with "space ships," but all it does is detract from the meaning of the bars. Avoid using vocabulary that you don't really know.

When Mike Tyson appeared on the Canibus track "2nd Round Knockout" (the LL Cool J diss), the high-pitched boxer talks about what Canibus should do. He says, "that's your name, Canibus, your whole objective is to eat emcees for lunch, dinner..." I'm pretty sure that Mike Tyson was confusing *Canibus* with *cannibals*. So don't be like Mike Tyson.

Use Medium-sized Words

Your vocabulary isn't just the SAT words you've got memorized, it's all of the words that you know. When you start out rapping, you'll probably find yourself writing lots of lines that feature 1-sylllable words. It's a fine place to start, and even veteran rappers often carve whole verses out of single and double-syllable words.

Just make sure you're not doing it too much. One and two-syllable words are great for flow and easy to spit, but they can be used to express only so much. When you want to really tell a story, or create something political, or battle, you're going to need to work in some medium sized words.

VOCABULARY

> **Pro Examples**
>
> *Its a new era in* rap *get* **use to it**
> <u>Kay</u> <u>Slay</u> *told me just do how* **you do it**
> *he said* Pap *If they spit fire then* **you fluid**
> — Papoose, "That's A Good Look"
>
> *A* **top-notch scholar** *with* **honors** *I'm so* <u>gifted</u>
> *live as the most vicious,* **honest** *and* <u>prolific</u>
> — Papoose, "The Beast"

The pro examples are two verses from the same underground emcee, Papoose. Notice the differences in word size between the two verses. In the first he's using lots of small words to flow. Every single word in those bars is only 1-syllable except "era" and "fluid", which have two syllables. The bars aren't bad, but I prefer the second verse.

In the second verse, which he spit on a Talib Kweli track, Papoose drops one word that you might not know ("prolific" meaning producing a lot of art), but generally he's just using medium sized words, and using them well. The words ("top-notch, scholar, honors, gifted, vicious, honest, prolific") aren't confusing. They add depth and clarity to his lines. Plus, he's using some amazing in-rhyming. Proving he's an emcee who spits fire, he out-raps Kweli on his own track, which, as you'll see in the next example, isn't easy.

In Battles

Battles are great places to drop some big words sometimes, because originality is so prized. It's hard to create a truly innovative punch using only the words "gun, bust, blast, shoot, dead," etc... It's much easier to create something original if you're using a word that most rappers don't use.

Again, be sure not to overdo it. Don't just flip the dictionary open to page 427 and start copying words into your verse. But when this technique is done right, the punches can hit hard, and it can have the crowd going wild. Take this amazing example from Talib Kweli.

> **Pro Example**
>
> You stoppin' us is preposterous like an androgynous misogynist,
> You pickin' the wrong time,
> steppin' to me when I'm in my Prime
> like Optimus, Transforming...
>
> — Talib Kweli, "Hater Players"

The first time I heard those bars, it was just like bananas in my ears. I had no idea what he was talking about. It was only after I listened a few times, that I realized how amazing those two bars are. In those two bars, Kweli drops a metaphor with wordplay (Optimus Prime was the leader of the Transformers on the old TV cartoon), a classic "you [doing something] is like

Vocabulary

[something unlikely]" punchline, and fills it with some wild vocabulary.

His punchline doesn't make any sense until you know what the words mean ("preposterous" means meaningless or absurd, "androgynous" means both male and female, and a "misogynist" is a woman hater). Kweli is basically saying, "you stopping us is meaningless like a woman hater who is part woman."

You definitely can't spit lines like that all of the time, but it's always smart in a battle to come with some unique, creative punchlines, and vocabulary can help you.

Practice This

Go to Flocabulary.com/wordlist and pick some big vocabulary words. Make sure you understand their definitions, then write them into some lines. Try to make it feel organic.

References

> **droppin' knowledge**
>
> *Let knowledge drop,*
> *Why should I be forced to*
> *play dumb?*
> *- Tupac,*
> *"Let Knowledge Drop"*

One problem with a lot of beginning rappers is that they rap about really vague subjects and repeat a bunch of played out phrases. You know what I mean? One cat I know is always just rapping about his nine, how he's tough, how he's rich. His rhymes are bad because he's obviously just biting a style, but they're also bad because they never really say anything. He's the kind of rapper that could rap for ten minutes and he's got you bobbing your head, but then at the end you can't think of a single line he said. You know the type? He never really makes the lines come alive. Take this example. The rhyming isn't terrible, but it's all really vague:

> *It's me dawg, ripping it up like this*
> *I kick it mad wild all night kids,*
> *my flow's tight you step to me? No not ever*
> *'cause I'm too hard to stop, I'll be rapping forever,*
> *and if you come by son, then I'm gonna rock,*
> *I'm hotter than the sun, and you know that you not,*
> *girls wanna get at, so they scream and holler,*
> *I'm making more money 'cause I get the top dollar,*

Now that wouldn't be so terrible as a freestyle, but as a written rhyme it's real weak. The worst thing about that rhyme is that it doesn't make any specific references at all. It just talks really vaguely about rapping and making money. There are no specifics whatsoever. Like I said this is a common problem for beginning emcees, but it's easily solved.

Improving Vague Lines

Take a line like this one: "I'm hotter than the sun, and you know you not." Saying that you're "hotter than the sun" is a very basic metaphor, and it's also kind of a cliché, kind of played out. We can make it much stronger by making it more specific. One way I can do this is I can figure out what specific part of the sun is hot. So, I'm going to go online and look up "the sun".

I went to Wikipedia.org (the online Encyclopedia) and this is some of what I found:

> "The Sun is the star at the center of Earth's solar system. It is the closest star to the planet Earth. Approximately 5 million tons of matter are converted into energy within the Sun's core every second, producing neutrinos and solar radiation. The Sun's magnetic field gives rise to many effects that are collectively called solar activity, including sunspots on the surface of the Sun, and solar flares."

So that gives me a lot more to work with. Now I can take specific parts of that information and try to make them into lines:

> *I'm hot like solar flares,*

or

> *I'm hotter than the star that's closest to Earth*

or

> *I'm hotter than radiation at the heart of the sun*

Any one of those works much better than the original line. While I was writing down "solar flares" I realized that it rhymed with "polar bears," which is interesting because solar flares and polar bears are basically opposites. One's hot, the other is cold. So I could probably carve a good line out of that. Something like this maybe:

> *Hold up there, stop it, 'cause I'm hot*
> *like solar flares, cool like polar bears when I rock it*

For the most part, the more intelligence and specific knowledge you can put in your lyrics the better. Specific references capture the crowds' attention and keep them listening. Sometimes a simple line works best, but too many simple lines is monotonous and boring like listening to George Bush try to talk about foreign policy.

Money vs. Currency

Let's take another example of improving a line:

I'm making more money 'cause I get the top dollar

It's another example of a weak, played-out line. It's also totally unspecific. Look how much better these lines are from some skilled rappers out there.

> **Pro Examples**
>
> *I'm making more green*
> *than that ni**a Saint Patrick*
> — Raw Digga, "Down for the Count"
>
> *They say money's the root of all evil*
> *but I can't tell,*
> *you know what I mean? Pesos, francs, yens,*
> *cowry shells, dollar bills*
> *or is the mind state that's ill?*
> — Talib Kweli, "Thieves in the Night"

So both rappers are talking about money, but Raw Digga puts in a clever metaphor comparing St. Patrick's colors to the color of money ('course now some money is pink and orange – somebody should rap about that!). Instead of just saying money, Kweli actually lists specific currencies from around the world. He even includes cowry shells, which are shells that were used for money in Ghana and elsewhere. They're both much better than some basic line about making money.

Do Research

Here's one more example of how to use specifics to make your verse better. Let's say you're writing a rap about how mad you are about the high price of gas. You could write something simple like this:

> *Gas prices sky high, fifty bucks to fill 'er up,*
> *'cause rich men who own gas won't ever give it up*

That's not bad. But I can improve it by making it a lot more specific. Again, I'm going to need to do some research. The internet makes it really easy. Wikipedia is a good starting place. It's a free online encyclopedia that users update. Since it's updated by users, the entries aren't always accurate, but for the most part people do a good job of regulating it and making sure it's accurate.

I'm going to do some research on oil. This is obviously going to give me a lot more than just information for my raps. It's going to educate me on the topic, and knowledge is power.

After I've done some reading, I can write a list of terms to potentially use in my rhymes:

Petroleum
Black Gold
ExxonMobil

References

Exxon Valdez
Peak Oil
Ethanol
Alternative Energies
OPEC (Organization of Petroleum Exporting Countries)
Carbon Dioxide
Greenhouse Gases
Global Warming

Now I can use those terms plus what I've read to carve out some really specific, dense lines to get my ideas across.

> *We're reaching peak oil, dawg, the point of no return,*
> *Limited oil reserves plus the globe's getting warm,*
> *I'm running on fumes while Exxon CEO's livin large,*
> *they use my taxes to pay for both sides of they wars,*
> *like to fight Russia we used to fund to the Taliban,*
> *now through OPEC, I'm paying for Iran contraband,*
> *I know what's up,*
> *they spill petroleum and don't clean it up,*
> *charge you hand over fist just for pissin' oil in yo cup,*
> *I'm giving all of it up, I mean it... I'm done,*
> *I need my car to run on corn, if u build it they'll come*
> *you wonder why no money goes*
> *to alternative energies,*
> *It's getting hot, but I've got AC blastin' in my SUV*

By having the knowledge and the vocabulary for what I want to say, it makes it that much easier to write raps with real content in them. Without knowledge, you'll never get past spitting simple raps, even if they are full of wordplay.

There are basically two types of references a rapper can use: historical references and cultural references. As their names indicate, historical references talk about something that happened years ago, while cultural references talk about something that happened very recently or is still happening. One subset of historical references is biblical references.

Historical References

Some of the emcees who use the best historical references out there are underground rappers. One of the best is Immortal Technique. His style is harder than most gangsta rappers, but he knows as much history as a historian. He manages to write hard-as-hell rhymes while dropping in references to the Council of Nicea, the Templar Knights, Paul Wolfowitz, Spanish Moors, and other stuff you've probably never heard of.

Check out some of these amazing lyrics, from his track "The Point of No Return," which I referenced in the first line of my oil rap. Basically, Immortal Technique is dropping a lot of knowledge. The lyrics are followed by a list of his references:

REFERENCES

> **Pro Example**
>
> *This is the point of no return and nobody can stop it,*
> *Malcolm Little when he knelt*
> *before Elijah Muhammad,*
> *the comet that killed the dinosaurs,*
> *changing the earth,*
> *they love to criticize, t*
> *hey always say I change for the worse,*
> *like prescription pills when you misusing them, ni**a,*
> *the Templar Knights*
> *when they took Jerusalem, ni**a,*
> *and figured out what was buried*
> *under Solomon's Temple,*
> *Al-Aqsa the name is not coincidental*
>
> Immortal Technique, "The Point of No Return"

References in those lyrics:

Malcolm Little is the original name of Malcolm X, before he decided to drop "Little" because it was given to his slave ancestors by their owners.

Elijah Muhammad was the leader of the Nation of Islam, a religious and political group that Malcolm X joined and became the most prominent speaker for.

A comet that hit the Earth is what many scientists believed caused the mass extinction of the dinosaurs millions of years ago.

The Templar Knights were an elite fighting force ("warrior monks") commissioned by the Catholic Church during the crusades. After **they captured**

Jerusalem from the Turks in the first crusade, the Templar Knights set up a headquarters on the Temple Mount, above King ***Solomon's Temple***.

Al-Aqsa is a mosque that is part of Temple Mount in Jerusalem. It's name translates as "the farthest mosque."

Biblical References

History books and the bible are both great places to go to pick up some intelligent references you can drop into your lines. One way to do it, is to read through history books and the bible until you get to a passage that really interests you. Then turn that fact or story into a few lines.

For example, most people know the biblical story of David and Goliath. The Philistine army marches into southern Israel to attack the Isrealites. Instead of straight up attacking, though, they set up camp. Their biggest (9'5") and meanest warrior, Goliath, challenges any member of the opposing army to fight. The winner of the duel wins the war and the entire opposing army. The only person to step forward is David, a young boy equipped with only a sling and some stones. Goliath attacks, but David shoots a stone into his eye. The giant falls to the ground. Then David takes the giant's sword and cuts his head off, thus saving Israel. David later became King David.

It's a good story, and it's become a piece of general knowledge, so it makes sense that rappers would reference it. Here are some examples. Ask yourself: who does it best?

> ***Tonedeff's slays giants,***
> ***as if my legal name's David,*** *what I say's blatant,*
> *no apologies necessary to glaze the game blazing*
> > -Tonedeff, "Heavyweights"

> *And I have been trying to be patient with they*
> *preoccupation with **David and Goliath**,*
> *but sooner or later, that patience gonna run it's*
> *course, and I'm forced to be a tyrant*
> > -Jay-Z, "Hovi Baby"

> *You get punched in the mouth with the southpaw,*
> *southern fist, I bust your sh**,*
> *swell your lip and get the Bubba shrimp,*
> *back to tougher sh**, what a wimp,*
> ***you giant Goliath brothers got shot with a***
> ***rubber sling***
> > -Canibus, "100 Bars"

> *That's the reason **your empire fell like Goliath***
> *I'm supplying the ghetto to satisfy you.*
> > -Cormega, "Rap's a Hustle"

> **Practice This**
> Choose a Biblical story that you like and write a line that references it. Try to use other techniques (wordplay, metaphors) as well.

Cultural References

In my opinion, Canibus won that bout. His reference to Goliath was tight, but it was even nastier because he preceeded it with a reference to Forest Gump: Forest's friend Bubba has big lips and loves shrimp.

Probably the best way to capture your audience's ear and get people laughing is to reference current events and today's culture. As I mentioned in the freestyle tips, the sooner you can mention something the better. These kind of references can range from Angelia Jolie giving birth in Africa to Bush not finding any WMD's in Iraq to the Boston Red Sox beating the Yankees on a certain night to the physical appearance of an American Idol contestant. We live in a media saturated culture, so you truly have thousands of things to pick from.

Ludacris is one rapper who uses dozens of cultural references in practically every song. Part of what makes his lyrics funny is his combination of wordplay and cultural references. In fact his song "Number One Spot" is a spoof on Austin Powers, so the song itself is referencing something. Take a look at some lyrics from that song.

> **Pro Example**
>
> *Explorer like Dora, these swipers can't swipe me*
> *my whole aura's so mean in my white tee,*
> *nobody light skinned been*
> *reppin' this hard since Ice-T,*
> *disagree, take the Tyson approach and bite me*
>
> Ludacris, "Number One Spot"

References in those lyrics:

Dora the Explorer is a cartoon character on a show aimed at preschoolers.

Ice-T is a rapper and actor who now stars on *Law and Order: SVU*.

Mike Tyson is a boxer who once famously bit Evander Holyfield's ear during a boxing match.

Another emcee who uses cultural references for humor is Eminem. He often writes whole verses discussing various aspects of pop culture. His song "Ass Like That," for example, references Triumph the Insult Comic Dog, Jessica Simpson and Nick Lachey's *Newlyweds* show, the Olsen Twins, Hillary Duff, Britney's Spears (who has "shoulders like a man"), Arnold Schwarzenegger, Janet Jackson's wardrobe malfunction, Pee Wee Herman, and Gwen Stefani. Eminem often combines references with wordplay, as with this example from one of his unreleased tracks, "Any Man":

> *Original Bad Boy on the case,*
> *cover your face*

> *came in the place blowed,*
> *and sprayed Puffy with Mase*

He's referencing Bad Boy label artists Puffy (Sean "Diddy" Combs) and his old rap partner Mase. The wordplay is on "mace," the stuff you spray muggers with.

Overall

Use cultural and historical references to add depth, humor, and interest to your lines. Keep your lines specific, not vague.

Other Techniques

> **droppin' knowledge**
>
> *"I would definitely say that when it comes to doing 16 bars, whether I am featured on somebody else's song or whether I am doing it myself, I am just not afraid to take it to the next level - doing something that I know no other artists would do - even with styling, metaphors or whatever. ...I want to be known as the most versatile MC out there."*
> - Ludacris

This section is for all the peripheral techniques, all the tricks of the trade not really big enough to merit their own chapter.

Alliteration

This is a simple technique that you probably learned about in English class when you were studying poetry, but it works well in rap. Here is the definition from the *American Heritage Dictionary*:

> **Alliteration** (*noun*) - The repetition of the same sounds or the same kinds of sounds at the beginning of words or stressed syllables, as in "scrolls of silver snowy sentences" (Hart Crane).

The Hart Crane example they gave uses a lot of alliteration (4 repitions of the "s" sound in six words), and some rappers do use it that much. But I'd mostly advise against it. Look at this example of a bar I saw some kid spit on the internet:

> *Simply stated, it's sad to say son,*
> *your stupid stories of soldiers*
> *that sold ya surpassed the second stage of stupidity*

Damn! That's like a tongue-twister. You don't have to make it so that every single letter is the same. Unless you're writing an alphabet song like Papoose or the Gift of Gab, you really don't need to overuse alliteration like that. When Rakim raps, "Nobody press up and mess up, the scene I set, I like to stand..." in "I Ain't No Joke", he's using alliteration subtly, but it adds a little something extra to the lyrics.

One of the direct descendents of Rakim's lyrical legacy is Nas, the Queensbridge emcee who combines a gangsta lifestyle with a poet's mentality. Nas' debut album, *Illmatic*, which hit airwaves and stores in '94, was practically an instant classic and immediately propelled Nas into superstar status. Check out the classy alliteration in his jam, "The World is Yours."

> *Pass the **m**argin to hold the **m**ic I'm throbbin,*
> ***m**echanical **m**ovement*

> *understandable **s**mooth **s**h***
> *that **m**urderers **m**ove with*

> **Practice This**
> Try to write an alphabet rap like the Gift of Gab or Papoose have done. Write a two lines where as many words as possible start with the letter A, then move on to B, etc...

Rhyming Sounds Repeated

While most rap verses use various different rhyme sounds, some of the illest verses out there have been written using one rhyme sound throughout the verse. Not only does it give your verse energy, but it shows off your skills. Check this verse from Raekwon the Chef on the bouncing Outkast joint, "Skew it on the Bar-B." Raekwon, a founding member of the Wu Tang Clan, never achieved the level of post-Wu fame that RZA, GZA, Ghostface Killah or O.D.B. achieved, but he definitely didn't dissapear. His solo debut, *Only Built 4 Cuban Linx*, secured his reputation as a deft storyteller and raw lyricist. He dubbed himself "Chef," because, as he says, "I'm cookin' up some marvelous sh*t to get your mouth watering".

Here's proof that he deserves the title. In this verse, he uses the "o" sound in "go" from start to end. He also works in other rhymes as well, including multies on "time grow" and "nine blow."

> **Pro Example**
>
> Deliver this through your **audio**, *ghetto mafioso*
> *grow hydro*, then bag it *up yo*
> price that longevity, suggest make moves ***slow***
> take **time** *grow* eight, react **nine** *blow*
> *hydro* slide *raw* like fu** *Renaldo*
> fly ride *though*, sh** lookin **wild** *dope*
> then **glide** *yo*, flippin the page, I *go*
> <u>watch</u> *five-oh*, jump on my meat, **ride** *slow*
> <u>watch</u> ***those***, undercovers, <u>cop</u> ***those***, <u>rock</u>
> ***those***, <u>glock</u> **blows** leave 'em baggy
> and collect <u>spot</u> **grows**
> Keep a <u>watch</u> **froze**,
> lean *on the* <u>yacht</u> and <u>wash</u> **clothes**
> Let the <u>chop'</u> **blow**,
> bag a half a <u>block</u> <u>plot</u> **grows**, what?
>
> Raekwon, "Skew it on the Bar-B"

A truly impressive verse both rhythmically and in terms of rhyme scheme. Note that Raekwon's using slant rhyme throughout ("blow" with "clothes"), which allows him to continually use the same sound and still put in some unexpected words ("audio," and "mafioso" for instance). He's obviously using a lot of in-rhyme (often on the 1, the first beat of the measure), and some wild multies ("watch froze" with "wash clothes"). He even sticks on topic, telling a brief story about growing weed and then having to bust out when the cops come. He does all of this so well that it conceals that fact that he sometimes repeats rhymes (he uses "grow" three times), which typically, you don't want to do. Raekwon finishes the verse with a "what," which is kind of like a surprise ending, but also makes the whole thing more badass.

Words Repeated

> **Pro Example**
>
> *I been pourin out some liquor for the fact that my pal's **gone**, and*
> *Tryin to help his momma with the fact that her child **gone***
> *And since we used to bubble like a tub full of Cal**gon***
> *Guess it's only right that I should help her from now on*
> *But since they got a foul on, what coulda **gone** wrong*
> *Now they askin Conse, how long has this **gone** on*
> *And maybe all this money mighta **gone** to my head*
> *Cause they got me thinkin money mighta **gone** to the feds*
> *So I ain't **goin'** to the dread, but he'll go'on up to bed, and*
> *When I came the next mornin he was **gone** with my bread*
> *And with that bein said, I had **gone** on my instincts*
> *And **gone** to the spots where they go to get mixed drinks*
> *But lookin back now shoulda **gone** to the crib, and rented*
> *"**Gone** With the Wind," cause I'dve **gone** about ten*
> *But I had **gone** with my friend, and we had **gone** to the bar*
> *And heard a ni**a talkin sh** so I had **gone** to the car*
> *And now the judge is tellin me that I had **gone** too far*
> *And now we **gone** for 20 years, doin time behind bars*
> *And since I **gone** to a cell for some petty crimes*
> *I guess I **gone** to the well one too many times, cause I'm **gone***
>
> Consequence, "Gone"

Though not nearly as famous as his cousin Q-Tip, the

rapper Consequence has left his mark on albums by TCQ and Kanye West. In fact, one of the most unique verses I've heard in a while is Consequence's verse on the *Late Registration* track "Gone." The song samples Otis Redding singing the word "gone," and Conse took this as a cue and wrote his entire verse featuring and playing with that word. In all he repeats the word 23 times in his verse.

The use of the word "gone" isn't random. It's essentially the theme of the song. Instead of spitting a verse about something random, Conse wrote specifically to the theme. Notice that he opens the verse using "gone" as the rhyme word, but then uses it exclusively for in-rhymes. He even finds some original phrases / words that have "gone" in them: Calgon, and Gone with the Wind. He also makes sure to finish the verse with the important word.

Visual Wordplay

This is a technique you can only use in text battles online, where your opponent and audience are reading your verse. Visual wordplay is any way that you call attention to the actual words you're typing: their shape, their color, what certain words spell. For example, you can color part of your verse red and then reference that like "i was seeing red like you when you're reading this line." You can also make the shape of your lines look like something (this is kind of like those old 'Christmas

Other Techniques

Tree' poems you used to write in the 3rd grade, where the poem itself is in the shape of a christmas tree). You can also spell out something with the first letter of each line. Take this example from EmceeBattleForum.com. I.B.I. is battling someone called Genocide:

Get the fu** outta here, GENOCIDE wants to battle?
Everyone know i.b.i's too much for GENO to handle
Now in lyrics 101, every tip you suggested-is-wack
Oh and dat Slim Thug pic, tha BOSS requested-it-back
C'mon man we all know ya dont flip-and-deal-white
I think ya only battle online cuz u cant win-in-real-life
Dood.... i cant lose..... cuz i.b.i wil never-die
Eternal destruction is comin, prepare for GENOCIDE

The reason he won that battle is that he used a clever concept and combined it with a dope verse. Be careful when you use visual wordplay, because your verses can sometimes end up looking stupid and corny. But occasionally, these tricks can work to add something new to a battle. Just make sure the verse can back it up.

Rhyming nonsense words

Use this trick in freestyles when you can't find a line or in raps to be funny. All you have to do is make up nonsense sounds and rhyme them (or don't):

> *I'm the lyrical monkey, oooh-oooh-ahhh-ahhh*
> *I make stinky diapers, gooo-gooo-ga-ga,*

That verse doesn't make much sense, but it's definitely unique. This is also the technique that Eminem uses occasionally for laughs, like in this song, "My Dad's Gone Crazy," one his best:

> *It's like my mother always told me:*
> *'ree-nee-ree-nee, ree-nee-ree-nee-ree-nee-ree-nee*

So do that.

PART THREE
PERFORMING

Guide to Flow

> ### droppin' knowledge
> *"Nah, that's definitely not enough. Wordplay and punchlines are just one little facet of emceeing. You gotta have the total package to be a great. I see a lot of kids nowadays with good lyrics and WACK deliveries. No flows...etc, etc. You need to be skilled in many different areas to be great."* – Tonedeff

It goes without saying that an emcee without flow is like Clark Kent without a telephone booth. Like Duke Ellington without that swing. Know what I mean? But what is flow anyway?

A rapper's flow is the way that he raps, the way that he enunciates certain words, puts emphasis on other words, puts words on certain beats or off-beats. Technically, flow is separate from the writing itself, so that two rappers rapping the same lines would have different flows. But since almost every emcee raps rhymes that he writes, flow and writing are closely intertwined.

Since flow is so personal and varies so much from

emcee to emcee, it's also one of the hardest things to teach. As you're reading through this lesson, the most important thing to remember is that your flow should be your own. You might copy Eminem's flow for a while as you're practicing and learning, but the goal in the end is to find your own flow, your own voice, your own style. All of the information here is just a starting block. It's up to you to take it farther and develop it into something amazing that no one's ever done before.

Before we go on, let's make sure we all understand what we mean by "line" and "bar," because I'm going to use these terms a lot in this section.

A bar is 4 beats

This is a little tricky because rappers and musicians use different definitions of the word "bar." To some rappers, a bar is two lines of a verse (i.e. one completed rhyme). To other rappers it is one line of a verse. To a musician, a bar has nothing to do with lyrics, it has to do with the beat. And this is the definition we're going to use.

A bar is the time it takes to count to 4 on rhythm in a song. This is only true of songs in 4/4 time signature, but that includes every single rap song I've ever heard. Typically the snare drum will hit on the 2nd and 4th beat in each bar. Most rap verses are either 8 or 16 bars long. A line is whatever lyrics a rapper spits over one bar.

Basic Tips on Flow

While every flow is unique, there are a few general things that you can do to improve yours.

1. Count Syllables

Counting syllables is the most basic way you can make sure that your flow is solid. The number of syllables in your line will depend on how fast you rap, but generally you're going to want between 10-16 syllables per line. You probably want most of your lines to match up in the number of syllables. Here's what can happen when they don't match up. These lines contain some good elements but are wrecked because of the flow.

> *My lyrics so good, God's reading them in heaven,*
> *plus you know I got more bars than the candy aisle*
> *in 7/11*

Here's the problem with that: there's way too many syllables in the second line. It breaks down like this: line one has 14 syllables. Line two has 18 syllables. That's not going to work.

But it's easy to fix. I'll just find 4 syllables that I can take out of line two without hurting the meaning of the line. First of all, we can take out the phrase "plus you know" from line two. That phrase is a filler anyway, and all it does is hurt the flow. That's 3 syllables gone, but I want to get rid of 1 more. So I'll change "the candy aisle" to "candy aisles," which gets rid of that extra syllable. Now we've got:

> *My lyrics so good, God's reading them in heaven,*
> *I got more bars then candy aisles in 7/11*

It's much better. Line one has 14 syllables. Line two has 14 syllables. The flow is much smoother. Whether they're conscious of it or not, lots of pro rappers keep their syllable counts the same from line to line. Here's an example from Chamillionaire's "Riding Dirty," a big single in 2006. Chamillionaire, a talented Houston rapper and teenage friend of Paul Wall, rose to national fame when Houston took over the hip-hop world in late 2005. Dubbed the "Mixtape Messiah," Chamillionaire made a name for himself with his deep, versatile voice and lyrical agility.

Line	**# of syllables**
Houston Texas, you can check my tags	9
pull me over try to check my slab	9
glove compartment gotta get my cash	9
cause the crooked cops try to come up fast	10

In these bars, Chamillionaire uses the same syllables

each time except for the last line when he goes double time on the words "cause the" leading into the line. (In fact, he is rhyming in double time throughout, but his syllables are still consistent). Putting the same number of syllables in your lines like Chamillionaire does will prevent them from being choppy and awkward. There are sometimes, though, when you'll want to use a different number of syllables in each line to mix it up. Just make sure you know that you're doing it.

2. Prominent vs. Silent

More important than the number of syllables is what kind of syllables you're dealing with. We've already covered what prominent vs. silent syllables are, check out the chapter on multies if you need a refresher.

Let's use the "Riding Dirty" lyrics from above and look at what stresses Chamillionaire puts on each syllable. Remember "/" means prominent or stressed, and "–" means silent or unstressed.

/ - / - / - / - /
Houston Texas, you can check my tags

/ - / - / -   / - /
pull me over try to check my slab

/   - / - / - / - /
glove compartment gotta get my cash

FLOW 103

$$- \quad - \quad / \quad - \quad / \quad - \quad - \quad / \quad - \quad /$$
'cause the crooked cops try to come up fast

He stresses almost all the same syllables in each line to make the rap come out smooth and uniform. The only exception is the last line, which has an extra syllable in it. I wonder if Chamillionaire's high school English teacher ever told him that he was rapping in trochaic pentameter, which is the metric opposite of the iambic pentameter that Shakespeare used. That's a little trivia in case you're ever on final Jeopardy and the subject is Chamillionaire vs. Shakespeare.

As you write your own raps, make sure that you're stressing similar syllables in each line. If you decide to break this pattern, make sure you're doing it for a reason. If you're not keeping track, your prominent and silent syllables can really mess up your flow. This simple example will show you what I mean. So some kid on the internet wrote these lines:

> *I'm gonna kill all and murder you especially*
> *I'll do it easily 'cause your not better than me*

He probably counted the syllables in each line and found out that there's 14 in the first line, and 14 in the second line. So he figures the syllables match so the flow will be dope. But he's wrong. Flow is about more than the number of syllables. Look what happens when we check out the stressed syllables. Pay close attention to the rhymes at the end of the lines.

> - / - / / - / - / - / - -
> *I'm gonna kill all and murder you **especially***
> - / - / - / - / - / - - /
> *I'll do it easily 'cause you're not **better than me***

You can see from the meter that these rhymes won't work. It's true that "especially" and "better than me" are rhymes, but they're bad rhymes because they're pronounced differently. You accent different syllables when you say them. In "especially," the "ly" is not stressed, but in "better than me" the "me" *is* stressed.

Don't rhyme a prominent syllable with a silent syllable. It makes the rhyme sound uneven. Not every single one of your lines with have exactly the same meter and speech pattern. That's okay. Just make sure that the rhyming syllables are stressed the same way.

Practice This
> Write out a rhyme and then mark the meter using slashes and dashes to analyze how you use unstressed and stressed syllables. Try to make sure your lines match up.

3. Breath Control

Ever heard those beginner emcees who have to gasp for air between lines? There's a reason you don't hear

Snoop Dogg doing that. He has breath control.

Breath control is actually closely related to the stressed and unstressed syllable count. The important thing is to make sure your words are evenly spaced and aren't too packed into the line. Unless you're Tonedeff or Twista, you shouldn't be putting 20 syllables in each line or you're going to run out of breath. Keep the syllable count closer to 14, and you'll ensure enough space to breath.

Your breathing doesn't always have to come at the end of the bar, but most of the time it will. In general, try to breathe from your diaphragm (your stomach, basically) not just your lungs. You'll get more air and more control over your air flow.

4. Rhyme Scheme

Where in the line you rhyme has a lot to do with how you flow it. For that reason, a tight rhyme scheme will always help out your flow. For beginners: keep your rhymes on the 4th beat of each measure (the second snare hit in most songs). Make sure that you're dropping a rhyme every-other time that snare hits. For more advanced rappers: use the in-rhyme and multi-rhyme lessons to switch up your rhymes. You can also take the rhymes off of the 4th beat, and move them elsewhere in the bar.

Speed

Fast

The speed with which you spit your rhymes determines your flow as well. Speed is usually measured by how many syllables you're spitting in each bar. Emcees typically drop 12-16 syllables per bar. As noted earlier, don't force it. Do what feels natural. And try to mix it up.

One example of some emcees who spit fast but keep it mixed are the two guys in Dead Prez, M-1 and Sticman. The two bring some wild lyrical stylings to their overtly political rap songs that tackle everything from the failing school system and police brutality to political propaganda and how radio stations try to control your mind. They're definitely worth checking out and studying closely.

> **Pro Example**
>
> Hip-hop *means* *sayin* what I want never bite my **tongue,** Hip-hop *means* teaching the **young**
> If you *feelin* what I'm *feelin* then you *hear* what I'm *sayin* cause **these** fake fake records just **keep** on *playin*
> What you *sayin* huh? ***DP*** <u>bringin the funk</u>
> Let the bassline <u>rattle your trunk</u>, uhhh!
> <u>Punk pig</u> with a **badge** wanna handcuff *me*
> cuz my pants they tend to **sag**
>
> Dead Prez, "It's Bigger Than Hip-Hop"

Check out the example from "It's Bigger than Hip-Hop". It's some wild stuff. The rapper M-1 uses lots of in-rhyme, lots of syllables and words, and a few multies. Where he really differentiates himself from other rappers, though, is how his rhyme scheme is all over the place. None of his rhymes fall on the same beat in the next measure. Instead, it's almost as if he's rhyming out of time.

He's also using lots of short words. He uses 68 total words in the four lines, and 83 total syllables. That's an amazing 20+ syllables per line.

Practice This
Write a few lines with 15+ syllables per line, where the rhymes do not fall on 4. The rhymes can happen anywhere you want, but don't put them at the end of the bar.

Slow

Some of the most talented emcees out there don't have the fastest flows. Don't equate rapping quickly with being a good rapper. A really talented rapper can rap at almost any speed and make it sound good.

As an example of a rapper with a killer flow who raps slower than M-1 or Eminem, let's check out some Jay-Z. Everybody knows that Hova spit some phat raps, with his one of a kind mixture of hard gangsta edge with that soft undertone and smooth delivery. Take a look at the lyrics from "Moment of Clarity," in which Jay-Z claims that he dumbs down his lyrics for his fans to sell more albums.

> **Pro Example**
>
> If skills *sold*, truth be *told*, <u>I'd</u> **probably be lyrically**, Talib **Kweli**,
> **Truthfully** <u>I</u> wanted to <u>rhyme</u>
> like Common ***Sense***
> (But <u>I</u> did <u>five</u> mill) <u>I</u> ain't ***been*** <u>rhyming</u>
> like Common ***since***
>
> — Jay-Z, "Moment of Clarity"

First thing you notice is that Jigga is using a lot fewer words than M-1 does. In these lines, he uses only 32 words and 44 syllables. That's just 11 syllables per line. He's basically using some really creative variations on the simple old school flow. But no one's hating on him for it. The slow speed make his lines easily understood, and his clever wordplay on "Common Sense (Since)" pops out. So do be afraid to rap slower, as long as you keep it tight.

> **Practice This**
>
> *Write a few lines with 10 syllables per line, where the rhymes fall right on the 4 (the second snare hit). Keep it simple, but try to make it sound phat.*

Imitate the Pros

One of *the* best ways to improve your flow is to listen to good hip-hop. Don't just listen to a rapper flow. Listen carefully. Listen analytically. Count the beats and figure out where he's putting each syllable and each word. Listen as closely as you'd listen to Jesus Christ and Martin Luther King, Jr. if they came over for dinner and started talking politics. Absorb every line.

A truly great flow exercise is to take one of your favorite rapper's verses, then write your own words to fit into his flow.

This is the technique that Eminem used when he released that song dissing Everlast (aka Whitey Ford from House of Pain). In a song on a Dilated Peoples album, Everlast raps "I cock my hammer, spit a comet like Haley / I buck a 380 on ones that act Shady."

He and Eminem had already had some disagreements, and so Em realized that Everlast was dissing him and talking about his daughter, Haley. Eminem came back at him with "Kill Whitey," a song that matches Tupac's famous Biggie diss track "Hit 'Em Up." Not only does Eminem's song match the beat, but Eminem and D12 match every single line of Tupac's song with one that sounds the same (same flow) but with mostly new words.

Pro Examples

*We keep on coming
while we running for you jewels,
steady gunning keep on bustin at them fools,
you know the rules,
Lil' Ceaser, go ask your homey how I leave you,
cut your young ass up, seen you in pieces,
now be deceased*
- Tupac, "Hit 'Em Up"

*I keep on coming
while you're running out of breath,
steady ducking while I'm punching at your chest,
you need to rest,
Dilated, go ask your people how I leave you,
with your three CDs nobody sees,
when they released*
- Eminem, "Kill Whitey"

Doing this with some of your favorite rapper's songs will not only give you a better idea of how they flow, and it will also improve your own flow.

Practice This

Choose a song with a flow that you really like and rewrite the song about a different or slightly different topic. Use the original rapper's flow.

A History of Flow in Hip-Hop

> ### droppin' knowledge
> "At certain times, it's just time to write, and it flows the way I want it to flow. It's almost like I get numb and it just happens. It's funny, man. I just try to stay at it and keep it popping, man.
>
> My style of writing, I love putting a lot of words in the bars, and it's just something I started doing. Now it's stuck with me. I like being read. The way you do that is by having a lot of words, a lot of syllables, different types of words." – Rakim

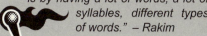

The History of Flow

The history of flow is really the history of hip-hop. From happy "wave ya hands in the air!" party tracks, to the dark portrait that Eminem paints when he's cleanin' out his closet, flow has changed as hip-hop music has evolved.

The next section explores some major movements in hip-hop music and analyzes a prominent, influential flow from each time period. In many of these movements, one rapper emerged with a flow that changed hip-hop forever. Of course, a lot of unique and important flows aren't featured here, but once again, we can't include everyone, so don't get upset. Also, we know that anytime you try to summarize something, you end up simplifying it and leaving truly important elements out. For example, when we discuss the Gangsta Era below, we don't mention the positive, jazz-inspired sound of the Roots that was developing at that time. There are always exceptions to any trend, and the brief history below should only be a starting block if you're really looking to learn about these and other artists.

The History of Hip-Hop + Flow

Years	Movement	Dominant Flow
1975-1981	The Birth	Coke La Rock
1981-1987	Old School	Melle Mel
1987-1993	Golden Age / Afrocentric	Rakim
1993-1996	Gangsta	Biggie / Tupac
1996-2004	Pop / Anti-Pop	Eminem
2004-now	The South	Big Boi / Ludacris

The Birth

Once upon a time in the early seventies, there was no such thing as a rapper, and the word 'MC' meant *Master of Ceremonies* and usually referred to a sleazy

A History of Flow

guy in a dinner jacket telling jokes at a stockholders' meeting. At this time in urban America, the DJ was the king of the club, the master of the party, but he rarely picked up the mic, and when he did it was never to rhyme. But then came one intrepid soul who (like that ancient fish with tiny legs that climbed onto land for the first time) picked up the mic, spit a rhyme, and changed history. His name was DJ Kool Herc.

Kool Herc, a native of Jamaica who had moved to New York City, brought with him the Jamaican practice of dub talking and toasting, which itself traced way back to Africa, to the griots or poets who told stories rhythymically over beats. Kool Herc began to add this element to the funk and soul beats that were hot in New York at the time. Originally, this was no more than Kool Herc yelling something like, "yo, this is Kool Herc, gonna make you work, put your hands in the air if you feelin nice." Much of the time, it didn't even rhyme. But as more and more cats came to check out what Kool Herc was doing, he began to bring two of his friends along to get on the mic to fire the crowd up: Clark Kent and Coke La Rock.

Fairly soon, these emcese had stolen the show. This was the time when emcees would spit for hours on end at parties in the South Bronx. The lyrics, which seem simple by today's standards, were exactly what the audience wanted to hear. Furthermore, an extremely complex flow wasn't desirable because in the age of live hip-hop (this was before any recordings), the audience had to be able to understand your lyrics the first time they heard them. This style or rhyming is what you hear on the Sugarhill Gang's Rapper's Delight, the first rap record (along with the Fatback Band's "King Tim III"). These rappers often rhymed nonsense words, creating a light party-happy style of music.

> **Pro Example**
>
> I said a hip, **hop** the *hippie* to the *hippie*
> the hip hip **hop**, a you **don't stop** the **rock** it
> to the bang bang *boogie*
> say up jumped the *boogie*
> to the rhythm of the *boogie*, the *beat*
> a *skiddlee* be**bop** a we **rock** a <u>Scooby</u>-Doo
> and guess what America, <u>we love you</u>
>
> Sugarhill Gang, "Rapper's Delight" 1980

Old School

From this foundation of African-American music emerged the rap innovators who truly shaped hip-hop. We call it Old School now, but at the time it was the most innovative, cutting-edge music in the world. These founding artists include Grandmaster Flash and Furious Five, the Treacherous Three, the Cold Crush Brothers, Afrika Bambatta, Kurtis Blow, and Run DMC. Of these, one of the most electrifying and influential lyricists was Melle Mel (pronounced Melly Mel), the lead rapper of the Furious Five.

A History of Flow

When you think of Old School flow, chances are you're thinking of Melle Mel. A gifted lyricist, Melle Mel was the first emcee to bring hip-hop away from the party anthems and towards something bigger. The Grandmaster Flash and the Furious Five song, "The Message," much of which Mel wrote, was the first socially conscious hip-hop song, paving the way for the a diverse group of 'conscious' artists.

Melle Mel's flow rides the snare drum like an expert cowboy on a bronco. He rarely falls off. His rhymes invariably fall on (or very close to) the snare kicks on the two and four beats, creating a foundation for rhyming that is still the norm today. When Big Boi or Eminem fly into their ridiculous flows, they are using the standard "Melle Mel" rhyme scheme as a launch pad. Oh, and don't think that Melle Mel's lyrics are simple. Check out the in-rhyme in his verse on The Message (*only* with *knows* with *grows* with *ghetto*).

Pro Example

A child is born with no **state** of *mind*
blind to the **ways** of man*kind*
God is *smiling* on *you* but he's frowning too
because **only** God **knows** what you go through
you'll **grow** in the **ghetto**, living second **rate**
and your *eyes* will sing a song of deep **hate**
the **places** you **play** and **where you stay**
looks like one great big **alley way**

Grandmaster Flash and the Furious Five
(emcee Melle Mel), "The Message" 1982

Golden Age / Afrocentric

Hip-Hop progressed in the eighties with various groups bringing unique talent to the table. And the rest of America (that is to say, white America) was finally paying attention too. Then in 1987, just as KRS-One and Schooly D were putting the gangsta in hip-hop for the first time (up to that point, rap music was often seen as a way out of gang life, not an expansion of it), a young poet named Rakim was sitting in his bedroom in a trance while his pen flicked across the page. He was writing what is largely hailed as the best rap album of all time, *Paid in Full*, while simultaneously ushering in an era of poetic, Afrocentric, conscious hip-hop, now known as the Golden Age.

Not only was Rakim rapping on new topics (he was soul-searching in his rhymes), he was brining a new flow to the game. His rhymes were still related to the Melle Mel Old School style, but he was now putting more syllables into his rhymes, he was using multies in his lines, creating lyrical textures that many emcees didn't even know were possible. The impressive flows of many of today's most talented artists would never be possible without Rakim laying down the groundwork. If you listen closely, you'll realize that the flows of Eminem, Mos Def, and Nas are direct descendents of Rakim's trademark style.

But more than that: the jazz and R&B-heavy sampling

of Rakim's partner Eric B. created a sound that influenced artists like Tribe Called Quest, De La Soul, the Roots, Tupac, and many more. In the early nineties, lots of rappers were connecting back with Africa, reestablishing their roots, and they had a whole new flow to do it with.

> **Pro Example**
>
> Write a *rhyme* **in graffiti in** every show **you see me in deep concentration** cuz *I'm* **no comedian,**
> jokers are *wild* if you wanna be <u>tame</u>
> I treat you like a *child* then you're gonna be <u>named</u>,
> another ***enemy***, not even a ***friend of me***
> cuz you'll get *fried* in the *end* if you ***pretend to be***
>
> Rakim, "I Ain't No Joke" 1987

Gangsta

Into this mix came the gangsta. Taking cues from Public Enemy, who had proved that hip-hop music could be a vehicle for anger and aggression, N.W.A. came *Straight Outta Compton*, ignoring PE's political edge and bringing the explicitness up a notch. Or two. Or four. For whatever reason, teenage white America made this ultra-hardcore music popular, and soon artists like N.W.A., Dr. Dre, Snoop Dogg, Tupac, Notorious B.I.G., and Mobb Deep had drowned out Afrocentric hip-hop.

In California, Snoop Dogg, Tupac, Ice Cube, Dre and others were pioneering that now-classic West Coast sound (built on funk-heavy seventies samples and unique synthesized instruments), and building a flow to match. Tupac's classic 'thug life' rapping style took Rakim's flow and added various rhythyms and some aggressive articulation. Tupac always attaced the mic.

Meanwhile, on the East Coast, The Notorious B.I.G. ignored the poetic techniques of Rakim, and instead founded his style on truly smooth delivery with wildly unique articulation and pronunciation. He and Tupac, despite their obvious differences, shared a powerful technique of occasionally slowing down the delivery of words in a line to make the bar phatter. Biggie was the opposite of a rap nerd or technician; he did it all by feeling, and did it with a delivery fans could feel.

Pro Example

Pink **gators**, my Detroit **players**
Timbs for my *hooligans* in *Brooklyn*
<u>Dead right</u>, if they <u>head right</u>, Biggie there <u>every night</u>
Poppa **been smooth** since days of **Underroos**
Never lose, **never choose to bruise crews who do** something to us, *talk* go through us
girls <u>walk to us</u>, <u>wanna *do us*</u>, **screw us**
<u>who *us*</u>? yeah, Poppa and *Puff*

Notorious B.I.G., "Hypnotize" 1997

Pop / Anti Pop

Biggie wasn't just a gangsta; he rolled with Puff "Man of a Thousand Names" Diddy/Daddy, who brought a

A History of Flow

blinged-out pop-friendly sensibility to the rap game. This ushered in an era of pop hip-hop, where the lyrics on the big records all had to be easy to follow. Jay-Z picked up where Biggie left off, while Will Smith got jiggy with it, and meanwhile Will Smith's music was sounding a lot like pop-sensations Britney Spears and the Backstreet Boys, who used hip-hop beats and production in their music.

This set the stage for satire, and the rapper to take advantage of it was a troubled young white kid from Detroit who had partnered with Dr. Dre. Eminem came out swinging. His music wasn't gangsta or conscious; it was something unique. Eminem put his dirty laundry out to dry in a way no other rapper ever had. Instead of yo mamma disses, Eminem invented the "my mamma" disses, aimed at his own mother.

With this, of course, Eminem brought a flow to the game that is second to none. He's so skilled with all of the various techniques in this book, it's almost as though he's just messing around, not taking it seriously. But he is taking it seriously. He spits multies so complex and subtle they would make Shakespeare's nose bleed. A trained battle rapper and talented freestyler, Eminem has set the bar high for the next generation of emcees.

> **Pro Example**
>
> All this **commotion emotions**
> run deep as **oceans exploding**
> Tempers *flaring* from *parents*
> just **blow 'em** off and keep **going**,
> not *taking* nothing from **no one**
> give 'em hell long as I'm breathing
> Keep *kicking* ass in the **morning**
> and *taking* names in the evening
>
> Eminem,
> "Cleanin Out My Closet" 2002

The (Dirty) South

You know that old post-civil war saying that white southerners sometimes mutter to themselves in dusty old bars: "the south will rise again"? Well, in hip-hop, it has. Lead by the success of Outkast and Ludacris, unique artists who added their own twist on typical dirty south style, southern rap is where the hits came from in 2005-2006. Among the big names are Goodie Mob, T.I., Outkast, Young Jeezy, Lil Jon, Ludacris (Atlanta), Triple 6 Mafia (Memphis), Mystikal, Juvenile, Lil Wayne (New Orleans), and UGK, Slim Thug, Mike Jones, Paul Wall, Chamillionaire (Houston). But the first southern group that anybody north of the Mason Dixon paid attention to was Outkast.

Outkast did it, and they did it with style. On first listen, the group seemed to have been formed randomly: Big Boi is a weed-smoking playa who raps about ladies and cadillacs, while wearing a baggy Falcons jersey. Dre (who later dubbed himself the *Andre 3000*), is more of a nerd. He spits rhymes about the ozone layer and finding lost childhood friends, while dressing in an "ascot to match the socks" and thick-rimmed glasses. But Outkast (who were friends since high school) proved that those two points of view don't have to oppose each other, they can complement one another.

It helps that both Big Boi and Andre have some of the illest flows in rap. Big Boi mixes a laid-back feel with fierce lyrical syncopation and vocal agility. He is a master of in-rhyme, and often takes the rhymes far away from the Melle Mel 2 and 4 flow, to put rhyming words all over the bar. He also stands out in the way he slows down certain words, spits others quickly, pauses, and then spits slowly again. With such an innovative and natural grasp on microphone control, Big Boi is definitely worth studying at length.

Pro Example

Sir Lucious got
gator belts and *patty melts* and Monte **Carlos**
And El **Dorados** I'm waking up out of my slumber
feeling like **Ralo, so follow** it's showtime at the **Apollo**
minus the Kiki Shepards what about a **ho** in a leopard-
print, Teddy Pendergrass cooler than Freddie Jackson
Sippin a milkshake in a **snowstorm** Left my **throat
warm** in the **dorm** room at the AU

Outkast (Big Boi), "So Fresh, So Clean" 2000

Hand Gestures

droppin' knowledge

Lady:
"John Paul, why don't you entertain us with something as well?"

Getti:
"Well, what should I do?"

Lady:
"Why don't you rap for us!"

Getti:
"No, I..."

Rockefeller:
"Come on old boy, I did mine"

Lady:
"It's so tribal!"

Getti:
"Oh, very well."

Lady:
"Oh goody!"

Getti:
"But hold my martini. I have to do those hand gestures."

- The Coup, "Pimps" (aka Freestylin at the Fortune 500 Club)

To rap is to tell a story in rhythm and poetry. And to get their point across, most rappers use their hands.

HAND GESTURES

Whether it's a loose-fingered wag or tight, staccato pointing, hand gestures add an important element to performing. Why do rappers use them? Hand gestures give your verses more energy, they work to emphasize certain words, and they add a visual element to a listening experience.

The first rappers used hand gestures to pump up a crowd at a party. Battle rappers use their hands to visually cut down an opponent. Freestylers often use hand gestures to help them concentrate and stay flowing. Most rappers have certain gestures that they use more often than others, but the best emcees have a full arsenal of eye-catching movements that they pull out whenver their verse needs it.

Lots of hand gestures that you'll see only feature one hand since the other hand is gripping the mic. Even when emcees aren't gripping mics (as in videos), lots of them stick to one-handed gestures and only use the other hand for certain flourishes.

The moves listed below are just some basic and common hand gestures used by various types of rappers. Using these as a starting point is good, but fundamentally you want to find something that you're comfortable with, something that is uniquely your own. Experiment with different styles until you find something you like that you can do easily and comfortably.

The Ninja Star

This is a simple classic that works for diverse styles, but especially for laid-back flows.

Drop your right arm to your side. Turn your palm up towards your face, and open it as if you were about to pitch a softball. Curl your pinky and ring fingers in to your palm, but keep your middle finger, index finger and thumb extended. As you spit, wag it back and forth. Some rappers keep their arm low, close to their hip, while others bring it up and extend it away from their body. The idea is that as you're flowing, you kind of look like you're tossing off ninja stars like that old Sega arcade game *Shinobi*.

Varation: the Kweli Finger Wag

This is the one used often by Talib Kweli. It's very similar to *The Ninja Star*, only more upright. Put your right hand in front of you, bending at the elbow so that your hand is just below your shoulder. Extend only the index finger and curl all others in. Keep your hand extremely loose and shake your wrist back and forth so that your hand wags. Occasionally throw your hand up in the air to mix it up.

The Common Off-a-the-Top-a-the-Dome Flick

Hand Gestures

This is the one used by Common and some other rappers when they freestyle. The idea here is that you want to show everyone you're freestyling by mimicking the motion of thoughts flying out of your brain.

Start with your right hand raised and the fingers lightly touching the right side of your forehead. This is also the position that some magicians use when they're trying to guess your card (though they close their eyes as well). Then, as you're spitting, your going to flip your wrist outward to mimic thoughts flying out. Keep your hand loose and wiggle your fingers as you're doing it. Then bring it quickly back to starting position, touching your head and repeat. Keep it natural.

Mess around with various rhythyms. The key to making this phat is finding a rhythym that works well with your verse.

You can go between this move and the *Kweli Finger Wag*.

The Mos Def You-Don't-Wanna-Mess Wave

Hand Gestures 129

This is a very simple move that shouldn't be overused because it's so repetitive. It's the one used by Mos Def sometimes to express disbelief and also by some battle rappers to say "don't step."

The arm is lowered but bent at the elbow so that the hand is shoulder-height. Your fingers should be extended and pressed together almost like a Miss America wave. Now angle your arm down a little so you don't look too much like Miss America and shake at the elbow. Works well with a corresponding head shake.

You can also add varation by angling your hand farther down. Try making it horizontal, almost like you're scratching a record. Once again, it's all about the rhythm.

The Slim Shady Chop

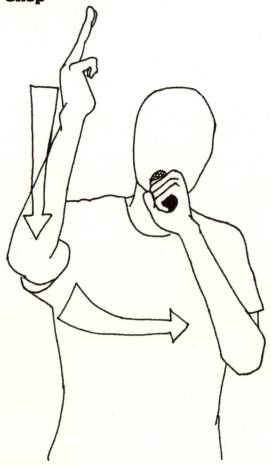

Hand Gestures

Eminem often raps with one arm extended far in front of him. He varies it up by throwing his arm in the air, dropping it to his side, swinging it back and forth or doing other moves, but his basic move keeps his arm far out in front.

Extend your arm in front of you so that your elbow is bent just slightly. Your hand can be pointing or with your fingers all flat. Now you have two basic moves. One is a vertical chop, up and down on the beat. The other is to twist your arm in front of your chest and either do something close to the Kweli Finger-Wag or just throw it back out again quickly. Because the motions are so dramatic and exaggerated, this one's good for big jams or battles.

I like going from this one into a full arm version of *the Mos Def You-Don't-Wanna-Mess Wave* and then back.

The Tonedeff Fast-Finger Piano-Playa

HAND GESTURES

Tonedeff is an emcee with an absurdly fast flow. He uses lots of unique hand gestures and adds lots of variation to match his wild, quick flow. One of his standards is the *Fast-Finger Piano-Playa*.

Your hand should be in the same position as with the Kweli Finger Wag, with your elbow bent and your hand extended. Instead of wagging, though, make the palm of your hand face the ground (or face front), and now bob your fingers up and down individually. Do this very quickly, as though you were playing a paino while riding a horse. This works best if you shake your hand back and forth sometimes, but then sometimes lift it up and down to the rhythm of your lyrics.

This is a really unique move that might not work for you, but it just shows that good hand gestures are as unique as the emcees who use them.

Videos / Add Your Own

We've got videos that show pro rappers using all of these hand gestures in their performances at www.Flocabulary.com/handgestures. You can also post your own favorite gestures. We'll pick the best ones and make illustrations.

Other Techniques

Bounce / Head Nod

A lot of the more energetic rappers aren't just moving their hands, they're moving their whole bodies. This is a must if you're doing a live show and you really want to pump up the crowd. Watch any video of a banging Tupac joint, and you'll see that he moves his whole body, using his hands only occasionally.

Tupac's standard move is different than a simple head bob. He bobs his whole body, bending at the waist or even at the knees. His head doesn't move independently from his body, it stays in synch. Occassionally, Tupac busts out with a ferocious hand movement: a pointing-gun, a *Slim Shady Chop* or another motion to highlight some of his hardest lines.

These are good moves if you've got a really banging beat. If you're rapping over something more relaxed or someone beat boxing, use these moves sparingly. Instead, rock some easy head-nodding.

Pantomiming

Another common hand gestures technique used by lots of emcees is to actually pantomime or act out something they mention in their lyrics. It's almost like they're doing charades. When done right and during the right lines, these pantomimes can make a visual connection with the audience or add power to a punchline at a battle. When done poorly or too often, you'll look like a French mime: corny and ridiculous.

Which hand gestures you use for your pantomimes really depend on your lyrics, but some common ones are: *the I'm-scribbling-on-a-pad* (pantomiming the act of writing), *the teeny-tiny* (two fingers close together), *the cash-rub* (rubbing the thumb against the fingers), *the gun-going-off* (a gun-point with the thumb hitting your hand like a hammer), *the drivin'-my-car* (one hand on the wheel), *the how-big-are-you* (good in battles, you point from your opponent's feet to his head, and then back to his feet), *and the rep* (fist to your chest or shoulder, reppin' your hood). Obviously, this is an incomplete list, and you should experiment with inventing pantomimes that match you're specific lyrics.

Move the Crowd

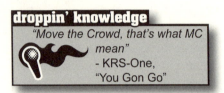

> "Move the Crowd, that's what MC mean"
> - KRS-One,
> "You Gon Go"

This is a small point, but it's worth making. As a performing emcee, you're goal is to connect with the people who have gathered together to hear you rhyme. The more you can win them over, the more you'll enjoy spitting and the more they'll listen to you. This is true whether you're in a cipher, on a stage, with your friends, or at a battle. Know them, and connect with them.

Know the Crowd

The first thing you need to do is to know you're audience. You'll probably spit different verses and in different ways if you're in front of friends vs. on a stage vs. online. If your goal is to win the crowd, you've got to know them first. Here's a little story to show you what I mean.

A few years ago I was at a Talib Kweli and Common concert in Philadelphia. The audience was mostly college kids and other people who were down with positive, so-called "conscious" hip-hop. After a few

Move the Crowd

weak opening acts, Kweli came out and the crowd went nuts. He did four or five songs and the crowd was really feeling it and having a good time. Then some guy came onstage and whispered something in Kweli's ear, and Kweli said, "ok, everybody, one of the opening acts got stuck in traffic. His name's J-Hook, and he just got here, so we're going to let him spit." The crowd wasn't really happy when this young cat came bouncing out. Then J-Hook started to spit.

Within seconds, the audience was booing him louder than Johnny Damon gets booed at Fenway. I looked around and saw a whole bunch of people with their fists up but their thumbs down. What had J-Hook done? He had spit a verse that probably would have won him praise at a battle. It was a hardcore verse all about "f-ing you up, f-ing your girl, shooting your moms," stuff like that. But that verse was the last thing people wanted to hear after hearing Kweli rap about elevating and respecting people.

J-Hook didn't even finish his verse. Kweli came out saying, "I don't know this brother from Adam," and then J-Hook threw his mic on the ground and walked off the stage. So don't go out like J-Hook. Know your crowd.

Connect with the Crowd

What do the best battlers do? They reference things

that they know the crowd is going to get. If there is an ice cream truck driving by when you're battling in the park, the emcee who references it in a clever way (with a metaphor, for example) is going to win a lot more points than the emcee who spits some nasty line he wrote earlier that day. When I worked in a restaurant, I used to freestyle after work with some coworkers and I'd rhyme about the different dishes we served. That always got them.

One thing that a lot of good performers do is talk directly to the crowd. I saw Mos Def performing once, and between songs he talked about how he liked hearing people call out requests. "We're not in the assembly line business, we're in the human interaction business." He went on, "if I feel a vibe to do something, I do it." The crowd ate that up. They could tell that he was committed to giving them a real experience and they appreciated it.

PART FOUR
BATTLING

Intro

Freestyle battling is a direct descendant of the African American oral tradition of playing the dozens. The dozens is a verbal game of insult swapping played among friends, acquaintances or enemies. Many credit the dozens with creating the "yo mamma" series of insults, though others argue that "yo mamma" jokes are as old as mothers themselves. (*On the sixth day God created yo mamma, and on the seventh day, He created yo mamma jokes*).

But freestyle battling has come a long way from casual back and forth disses. The best battlers of today create rhymes that are lyrically immaculate but pack enough punch to knock a dead horse back to life. This section is divided into a general Guide to Battling, which outlines all of the important elements of winning a freestyle battle, and a section on Punchlines which focuses on specific types of punchlines, since punches serve as the backbone of any good battle verse. Keep ya gloves up.

droppin' knowledge

"I kind of discovered battling like accidentally you know. I didn't really know about it. When I was in my first battle I guess like in junior high, just like in the cafeteria it just turned into a battle and I wasn't really sure what it was but the guy started dissing me and we were going back and forth and I lost actually, but that's when I figured out what freestyle battling is.

I guess it went through different stages because at first it was something I did for fun and I thought it was a good way to express myself and you know like after a battle you get your props, you get respect and that's what kind of carried me to the next stage which you know as I was thinking that I wanted to do this as a profession, meaning get a record deal and stuff like that. Then I was thinking you know what, battling is a good way because you know what better way to get credibility than battling and eating MC's up."

– Jin, Freestyle Battle Hall of Famer on 106 & Park

Guide to Battling

1. What is a freestyle battle?

In the most basic sense, a freestyle battle is any two people rapping live and trying to diss each other. A battle can be formal and have rules (a certain number of bars, or a certain time length), or it can be informal, just two people dissin' back and forth. Some battles will have a 'winner,' decided upon by votes, but most informal battles won't have an official winner. Still, even in an informal battle, most people will know who came stronger.

Beyond just dissing someone else, though, whenever you battle rap you should push yourself to make your rhymes as quality as possible for your own sake. The purpose of any battle is really twofold: to beat your opponent and to improve as a rapper.

2. What's the key to winning a battle?

The key to winning a freestyle battle is this: win the crowd. The rapper who wins the crowd over, wins the battle itself. Simple as that. One rapper might come harder, and the other might spit more clever punches, but the winner will always be the one who connected with the people, the rapper who gets them *oohing* and *ahhing* and screaming "oh damn!".

The best way to get the crowd on your side is to spit a verse that is full of clever, hard-hitting punches. Those are the lines that most crowds will respond to the most.

3. What are punches?

Punches are any phrases in your verse that diss your opponent. Punchlines are lines that contain punches. Punches can be general, broad attacks ("No skill, lil' boy, you totally wack,") or personal ("read my mind, did your mama cut your hair, or is your barber blind?"). But they should always hit hard.

Think of a freestyle battle like a boxing match. All the fancy wordplay and sick flow is just you bobbing and weaving. It's important. You might sound good, and people will feel it, but you can't ever win the battle and knock out your opponent if you don't throw a few good punches.

Compare these examples:

> *The tightest flow on the planet to prove I'm the best,*
> *I'm the illest king of the land, ruling all the rest*
> (no punch)

> *The tightest flow on the planet to prove I'm the best,*
> *Yo flow's like thick mucus that get caught in yo chest*
> (broad punch)

My flow's tight like your shirt, how can you breathe?
Yo shirts got the right idea, I think it wants to leave
            (personal punch - if your opponent is wearing a tight shirt)

4. How many punches should I put in my battle?

Ideally you want every or every other line to be a punchline. So if one line isn't a punch, it should be building to one, setting one up. If you were to map a battle verse visually, it would look like waves, where the crest of each wave is the punch. The lull in between the waves builds the audience's anticipation, but you never want to let too much time go by without delivering another carefully-honed attacked.

Take the battle in *8 Mile*. Eminem's character Rabbit is battling a dude named Lickity Split. This is part of Lickity Split's verse. Though he ends up loseing to "Rabbit", he comes with a pretty hard verse. Let's analyze the punches.

You ain't Detroit, I'm the D
            (weak semi-personal punch)
You're the New Kid on the Block
            (leading to...)
'Bout to get smacked back to the boondocks
            (personal punch, but not hard)
Lil' Nazi, this crowd ain't your type
            (leading to...)

BATTLING

Take some real advice and form a group with Vanilla Ice
                              (semi-personal punch)
And what I tell you, you better use it
                              (no punch)
This guy's a hillbilly, this ain't Willie Nelson music
                              (semi-personal punch)
Trailer trash, I'll choke you to your last breath
                              (broad punch)
And have you lookin foolish
                              (leading to...)
Like Cheddar Bob when he shot himself
                              (personal punch)
Silly Rabbit, I know why they call you that
                              (leading to...)
Cuz you follow Future like you got carrots up his ass crack
                              (hard personal punch)
And when you actin up that's when you got jacked up
                              (personal punch)
And left stupid like Tina Turner when she got smacked up
                              (broad punch)
I crack ya shoulder blade, you'll get dropped so hard
                              (leading to...)
that Elvis will start turning in his grave
                              (weak personal punch)
I don't know why they left you out in the dark
                              (leading to...)
Ya need to take your white ass back across 8 Mile to the trailer park
                              (personal punch)

As you can see, every line was either a punch or leading to one. Overall, it was a solid battle verse, though he did make some mistakes, which is why he ultimately lost. First of all, his punches were all basically dissing the same thing: Eminem is white / he doesn't live in Detroit. The broken record approach is not a successful battle technique, like a basketball player with only one shot. The reason that Michael Jordan or Lebron James are so lethal on the court is because of how versatile they are. They're threats from 3-point range, and they're threats with an inside lane. By sticking to basically one topic, Lickety Split opens himself up to Eminem, who can now easily flip the one-dimensional disses back in Lickety's face.

5. How should I use broad punches?

To my mind, broad punches are over-used, but they do have their place. Broad punches are anything that you could spit to one emcee just as easily as you could spit it to another. These rhymes are easy to write beforehand, unlike specific punches. It's a good idea to write some broad punches that you can pull out whenever you get stuck, or weave into your battle rap between personal punches.

Since broad punches don't hit as hard as personal attacks do, make sure that your broad punches are funny, intelligent, or lyrically impressive. Compare these:

BATTLING

> *I'm only battling ya*
> *to prove the point that you a sell out,*
> *so when I come round with the ak and 9 out,*
> *yo its lights out*

This broad punch is weak. There's no metaphor, no vocabulary, no wordplay, no multies, and it rhymes "out" with "out" with "out." The only punch in there is a gun punch, and gun punches are played out. They're rarely creative, and weak rappers love 'em. So put your imaginary AK and 9 back in your pants and spit something real. Check this out, from a Texas rapper named *smtxgraffin*, writing on the internet:

> *Why do you spit corny punches that nobody understands?*
> *You ain't in my league, I'm pitchin' at you underhand*

This is a broad punch (it could be specific if his opponent is spitting truly corny punches), but it works because of the play on "league" and the creativity of the line "pitchin' at you underhand." Plus "understands" and "underhand" is a dope rhyme.

In general, use broad punches sparingly, and when you use one, make sure it's tight.

6. How should I use personal punches?

Personals are the bread and butter of the veteran battle rapper. Not only do they cut down your opponent, but because they are basically impossible to write beforehand (unless you know who you're battling the night before) they show off your freestyle prowess. Use personals as much as you can in your battle raps.

7. How do I write personals?

Here's the trick: as soon as you know who your opponent is going to be, start analyzing him and breaking him down. If you're at a contest, as soon as they announce your match-up, find out which guy is going against you and take a look at him / ask about him. If two emcees are battling at a party and you want to jump in, figure out who you'll be battling. If you're battling in an online forum, as soon as you know who you're up against, go and read a bunch of his old battles and old posts. You want to dig up as much info as you can that you can use in your raps. In the example from 8-Mile above, Lickety Split disses Eminem in these personal ways:

*he's not from Detroit
*his friend Cheddar Bob shot himself in the foot
*his friend Future hosts the battle
*he's white
*he lives in the trailer park
*he got beat up by a bunch of Lickety Split's friends

That's a lot of personal information that Lickety Split used against him, even if most of his attacks were too similar. In general the more you can find out the better. A good place to start is superficial details: what he's wearing / his name / what he looks like. Let's say the guy you're battling is wearing two hoodies on top of one another:

> *Couldn't decide which shirt to wear so u wore both G?*
> *U could wear 6 shirts and u still won't hold the trophy*

8. Preparing for the battle beforehand

Not every battle is a freestyle (think of the diss wars between Tupac and Biggie or Common and Ice Cube). All those artists released written diss raps to battle their opponent. Plus, even at a lot of freestyles, cats spit pre-written raps, though they often get called out. I would advise against spitting an entire pre-written verse at a freestyle battle. Everyone's gonna tell it's pre-written anyway, and they're more likely to give props to someone who put in at least a few freestyle bars. But you can always use some pre-written elements.

If you watch the special features on the 8 Mile DVD, there's one scene where Eminem battles this woman (an extra in the movie). He appears to be freestyling when he spits, "so you a dope emcee? Don't be mad and start taking your period out on me." The audience goes wild. It seems that Eminem just freestyled an amazing, personal punch.

But there was something about that line that sounded familiar to me. I walked around for a few days, trying to think of where I had heard it before. And then I realized that Eminem wasn't biting another rapper's lines; he was recycling his own. The "PMS" punchline was the same line he used against a girl in the Rap Olympics in 1997. So what had he done? Sometime before the Rap Olympics he had written that line as a punch in case he went up against a woman. He used it in the Olympics and then, five years later he pulled it out again to beat an extra in his movie.

The trick was that he made it sound fresh both times. He spit it mixed in with his freestyle, and he spit it in such a way that it seemed like he made it up on the spot. That's something that a truly talented emcee can do: rock a pre-written line like freestyling. The trick: don't spit too complex a line, and pause a tiny bit (like you're trying to think of the line) before you bust it out

It's a good idea to do what Eminem did. Write out a bunch of specific punches before a battle and memorize them. Then you can use those rhymes if you ever find yourself up against someone who fits that description. Here are a bunch of basic categories:

Battling 151

*someone who is skinny / fat / short / tall
*someone who is spitting a whole pre-written verse
*someone who is old / young
*someone who is closed minded / racist / sexist
*someone who wears glasses / a hat / a bandana
*someone who has long hair / short hair / dread locks / is going bald
*etc...

Practice This
Write a few really dope punches for each of these types of people. Practice sneaking them into your rhymes while you're freestyling. Then you'll easily be able to drop them into your battle verse if you come up against an opponent who matches the description.

9. The second rapper should respond to the first

Someone always has the unfortunate job of going first in a battle. This is defintately the weak spot to be in, which is why it's usually reserved for challengers. There are two major drawbacks to going first: it's harder for the audience to remember your punches at the end of the battle, and the other rapper can use your punches against you. As the first emcee in a battle, it's up to you to spit something hot enough that the audience will remember it. Try to get the crowd as involved as possible. You want to get the crowd on your side to intimidate your opponent. As legendary rapper Kool Moe Dee says, "cheers for you are boos for your opponent."

But it's difficult for the second rapper too. As the second rapper, the audience expects you to respond to the lines and punches that your opponent has just leveled at you. You've got to answer him directly. So if you're opponent called you a lazy Mexican, it's up to you to flip that around in his face.

This is true for everyone, but it is especially true if someone took a cheap swipe at your race, background, gender, etc... It's easy to expose them on the flip side. Check out this example from BET's *Rap City*. This battle features Jin, the battle champion, who is of Chinese descent, versus a challenger, Sean Nicholas.

Sean Nicholas spits first, and immediately goes after Jin's race:

> *Who you supposed to be?*
> *Bruce Lee with his pants all saggin'*
> *I'll murder you boy,*
> *There'll be no return of the Dragon*

It's a clever punch, but it's the only one he has in his whole verse. He goes on to say that Jin, dressed in orange, looks like Tony the Tiger, but then he blanks. He just can't think of a rhyme for "Tony the Tiger." Instead of just saying something random, he pauses awkwardly, and doesn't finish the rhyme. At that moment you know that he's got to come back

BATTLING 153

with something hard to make up for his embarrassing mistake, but instead he resorts to a seemingly random bout of toasting (rapping in a Jamaican accent), until the DJ cuts him off.

Jin picks up the mic and is quick to turn the tide, shoving the guys comments (about how he dresses and how he's Chinese) back in his face.

> *You're not a record artist, I'm not hating on you,*
> *Stop lying, Miss Cleo is more Jamaican than you...*
> *My pants are new, my sweater is new,*
> *Don't be mad a Chinese kid dress better than you,*

Jin responds to his opponent and tears him apart. He references specific things from his opponent's verse, letting you know that he wrote the lines right then. The fact that Sean Nicholas went first allowed Jin the time to write out those killer punches. As soon as Sean Nicholas started toasting, Jin probably thought, "ok, he's rapping in a Jamiacan accent. What else is Jamaican that I can make fun of him with? Miss Cleo!" And then he worked that idea very quickly into a line. This is an important strategy that all battlers should use.

Note: if you're battling someone online, some websites don't allow you to use your opponents lines against them (they think it gives the second rapper too big an advantage). Make sure you know the rules first.

10. Use your body / Act it Out

At a battle you are a performer, and a performer doesn't win the crowd by standing there like a stiff with his hands in his pockets. You've got to energize the crowd through movement. While hand gestures usually accompany any live verse, skilled battle rappers will bust out some extra-powerful gestures that help their punchlines hit home.

First of all, you want to move around enough to get the crowd pysched. Don't stand there like a poindexter. You don't have to be jumping around the stage, but at least move your upper body as you're rhyming. Then, as you're dropping you're lyrical missiles on your opponent, you want to emphasize them with motion. A lot of this will depend on your style and on the verse you drop, but a good starting place is to point to your opponent with your full arm extended every time you say "you" in your verse. If you diss their shoes, always point at their shoes. If you diss their beard, either point at their beard, or scratch your own chin like you've got a beard. These visual clues will help the audience connect with your verse.

You can check out some free videos at *www.EmceeBattleForum.com/rapbattlevideos* to see how the pros do it.

BATTLING 155

11. Yo, that dude just dissed me. That means war, right?

A battle is a competition, not a war. Just 'cause a rapper says something about you in a battle doesn't mean you two are now enemies. NBA players on the court don't hate each other. They always try to beat their opponent, but then they shake hands and say 'what's up' after the game. I like an opponent who says, "good battle" after we spit verses. You never know, you might want that guy to join your crew someday, or you might join his. In anything, but especially in the rap game, it's always better making friends than making enemies.

12. How should I start and end my verses?

Like any relay-race or three paragraph essay, you want your strongest punches to come first and last (with emphasis on the last). You want your battle verse to open with a strong punch to get the crowd on your side. Take this example from Masta Ace on "Acknowledge," a diss track against a rapper named Boogieman. Masta Ace opens with a strong name diss, which we'll cover in the next chapter.

> **Pro Example**
>
> Yo I heard of the Boogie Man
> when I was a youth… Scary…
> Then I found out that he was as fake as the tooth-fairy
>
> Masta Ace, "Acknowledge"

That's a strong opening punch, personal and clever. Start strong like that and then try to end your verses with a strong punch as well. Ideally it's one that sums up some of your lines, or provides some closure. Compare these endings:

> *I'm the rap vet, spit lines that most people can't get,*
> *my lyrics destroy yours like the Yankees vs. the Mets*

This is a pretty weak ending. The punch is fairly weak and it doesn't really sum anything up. Try this one:

> *So can you write down your lyrics*
> *and give me a copy soon?*
> *I need 'em dog,*
> *cause they're out of toilet paper in the bathroom*

This works much better as an ending. The "so" works like an "all in all" or "in the end," a phrase that let's people know you're about to end, and the punch hits hard. It's good to end with something clever and funny that the audience can appreciate.

13. What should I avoid?

Don't fall victim to what I like to call LL Cool J Syndrome. You know you've got it if your whole battle verse is all about how ill you are on the microphone, how ladies love you, how you're so rich, or how chromed out your car is. In LL's famous battles with Kool Moe Dee, Ice-

T and Canibus, the buff rapper spent more time self-aggrandizing and band-standing then actually dissing his opponents. As Kool Moe Dee himself instructs: "focus on you opponent, not on yourself... crystallize their weakness."

You should also avoid any punch that's been played out, and there is a lot of battle material that's been played out bad. A lot of cats still spit stuff like this, so it should be pretty easy to beat them. I like to come to a battle with a few lines that take a swipe at homophobic, gat-loving, sexist rappers in case I go up against one. Closed-minded rappers will never get to the top.

Avoid:
    *faking in general – you're going to get called out
    *rapping about sexual exploits – everyone knows you're lying anyway
    *using the word "gay" or "faggot" – played out and stupid
    *dissing on women – idiotic
    *being racist – you're going to get called out
    *talking about your gat – you don't really have a gat, dawg.
    *dissing yo' mamma – only to be used occasionally

14. Are there any other tricks?

One of hip-hop's most interesting beefs was between Ice Cube and Common back in the nineties. Common came out with a track on his album *Resurrection* (Relativity, 1994) that told the history of hip-hop music. The song, "I Used to Love H.E.R." personifies hip-hop as a beautiful but abused woman who has traveled from the East Coast to the west and back again. Apparently, former N.W.A. member Ice Cube took exception to Common's lyrics and blasted at him with a few potent diss lines on a Mack 10 track, "Westside Slaugherhouse." Common then fired back with the diss track "B*tch in Yoo."

Ok. Now pretend for a minute you haven't heard any of these songs (maybe you haven't), and just pick a winner based on who you imagine would win a battle. The contest is between hard-as-nails, west coast gangsta Ice Cube and nerdy poet Common. Most people pick Cube, right? Well that's exactly why Common won the battle. His diss track "B*tch in Yoo" wasn't insanely angry like one of Tupac's endemics. It wasn't lyrically nasty like Canibus dissing LL Cool J. Instead, it played to all of Common's strengths: it was a poetic, interesting, soft-spoken attack that dismantled his enemy piece by piece, accusing Cube of being a hypocrite, a smart rich man fronting like a gangsta. Common won the battle because he didn't front. He kept the track true to himself. In other words, if you're a screamer then by all means, scream. But if you're more of a lyrical poet, then bring that same focus to your battles. Use your strengths to defeat your competitor.

BATTLING

Make your battle raps as dope as the rest of your raps. Include metaphors, word play, similes, cultural references, multies, and weird rhymes. Always push yourself to battle as best you can. You're going to lose at some point, everybody loses. Learn from your losses and come back stronger next time.

In Summary

- *as soon as you find out who you're battling, learn about him / analyze him
- *find some details you can exploit,
- *write some personal punches using those details, "crystallize their weakness"
- *mix in some pre-written punches
- *outline your rap with strongest punches first and last
- *if you go second, respond to your opponent's verse
- *spit fire
- *give your opponent a dap and say 'good battle'
- *win or lose, you'll come back harder next time

Punchlines

droppin' knowledge

"A good punchline will never go out of style. That's all you need. A good punchline let's you know where that person's mind frame is – what they know, what they're aware of." - Skillz

"In a battle, punchlines are your offense, and wordplay is your defense."
- Jhonny Blaze

Punchlines are definitely the most integral part of a battle verse. The previous chapter discussed punchlines at some length, but they're important enough to merit even more attention.

Three Common Problems with Punchlines

1. Too General / Played Out

I mentioned this in the last chapter, but it's important enough to highlight once again. If your punches are general (i.e. they could be applied to anyone), then they better be tight as hell. And if you're talking about stuff that everyone talks about, then you better have a new way of saying it. If all you're spitting is: "you're gay, fu** you, I fu**ed your b*tch, you suck, I'm dope, I shot you, I'm rich," just stop. Your verse is wack. Don't treat your verse like that. You better love your verse like it was your own baby. You know what I'm saying? Breast feed your verse. Yeah, I said it. So what? Spend some time on your verse, and come creative and innovative and hard as nails.

2. Don't Mess Up Your Flow Trying to Fit in a Punchline

I've lost battles for this very reason, and it always sucks. The trick with using any punchline is not to disrupt your flow. If you're writing a verse and a certain punchline fits, then use it. But if you have to change up the whole flow of your rhyme to fit it in, you're better off finding something else. Here's an example of a punchline tripping up some cat's flow:

> *Oops you're dead, just shot your head,*
> *you should pass the microphone to your team like Jason Kidd*

The first line isn't bad, but the second line seems stuck on randomly. The second line is much longer than the first (it has 14 syllables, the first has 7). The whole thing comes off as uneven. Avoid that.

3. Don't Overwrite Punches

A common problem among smart beginners is to overwrite their lines. It's a thin line to walk. You want to make sure your lines aren't boring and simple and played out, but you can't spit obscure references or convoluted rhymes. You don't want to be stupid, but you can be too clever too. Check this:

You couldn't en-'Tyse' 'Mikes' if you won at 'Punch-Out'

So that line is referencing the old Nintendo boxing game, *Mike Tyson's Punch Out!* But the line barely makes sense. It plays with the word "entice," but "entice mics" isn't a saying. It doesn't really mean anything. It's wordplay, but it isn't funny or very clever. When you're stretching it that far, it's time for a rewrite or a whole new line. Here's another example of what you should avoid at all costs. Let's say I'm battling someone on the net, and I drop this:

> *You know who I am,*
> *the one these players love to hate,*
> *I discuss first cause in my first clause like*
> *the Saladin-Gish debate**

> **In 1988, the Dr. Kenneth S. Saladin and Dr. Daune T. Gish debated the theory of evolution. In the first clause of Saladin's argument, he made reference to the old thirteenth century "First Cause" argument, which states that everything must have a cause.*

Ok, here's a general rule: never, ever, ever include a footnote to your raps. A battle verse shouldn't be like

PUNCHLINES

a treatise on oceanographic currents in the Byzantine Empire. If you have to include a footnote, then your punchline is never going to hit as hard as it should. Rewrite it. Another rule: if you're going to reference something smart, make sure people understand the basic idea of what you're talking about.

This is cool:
I'm like Zeus throwing lyrical lightning bolts

But this is not cool:
I'm like Hephaestus, cuz my arts too crafty*
(*Hephaestus was the Greek god of arts and crafts.)

You can drop that as a joke, but not as a serious punch. You'd get laughed off the stage. So overall: spit smart, but don't overwrite. And don't include footnotes. Battles are supposed to be between two opponents spitting live on a stage or a street corner or in a living room. There are no footnotes in real life.

Popular types of Punchlines

Use this list of popular types of punchlines to get ideas on forming punchlines, but also be careful. If a punchline has made this list, that means it's been covered a lot. If you're going to use one of these types of punches, make sure to use them creatively, otherwise your punchline is going to sound like news from the day before yesterday.

Wordplay Punchlines

Like I mentioned in the previous chapter, punchlines with wordplay are often some of the most effective and interesting lines you can drop. Not only do they diss your opponent, but they show off your lyrical skills and get the audience laughing. Check out this example from Wordsworth on "Twice Inna Lifetime":

> *In rhyme battles, you'll dial nine,*
> *just to get a line out*

Wordsworth is referencing the fact that in most office buildings or schools you have to dial "9" on phones before you make a call outside the system. This kind of punchline isn't the hardest punch in the world, but it will always win you points with the crowd, which is the key to winning. Do your best to make something that both disses and is truly clever. Consult the Wordplay chapter for more on how to create rhymes with wordplay. Here's one more example from B-Ghutta on EmceeBattleForum.com:

> *Ok prophet,*
> *you done stepped into the wrong domain...*
> *So i'll just Kill u in the first two lines*
> *like some strong cocaine*

As discussed in the Metaphors chapter, B-Ghutta is using a metaphor with wordplay, a killer combination.

The "you couldn't _____ if you _____ " Punchline

One of the most popular types of punchlines are the "you couldn't _____ if you _____" punches. These punchlines almost always involve wordplay as well. For example:

> *You couldn't spit fire if you had lighter fluid saliva*
>
> *You couldn't rock if your mom was granite / your pops was quartz*
>
> *You couldn't play me if your middle name was Atari*
>
> *You couldn't hit me if this was Blackjack and you was the dealer.*

This is a really popular type of punchline (they're used all over the internet). These punches can be very effective when done correctly, but they can also come out corny, stupid and awkward. As with all punchlines, just make sure they don't mess up your flow and they're not overwritten. When done right, though, these punches hit hard.

Make sure to mix it up. There are lots of variations on this type of punch that you can use. You can easily change "you couldn't" to "you wouldn't, you can't, you won't, you aren't."

The "you [doing something] is like [something unlikely]" Punchline

A variation of the "you couldn't blah if you blah" punch is the "you [doing something] is like [something unlikely]". These punchlines are usually unique enough that they don't need any wordplay. But they almost always involve historical or cultural references.

> *You rocking me is like Jessica Simpson finding the cure for cancer*
>
> *You winning this is like Mr. Rogers singing "I hate kids"*

Those lines work fine by themselves, but you can also explain what you mean in the next line. Like this example, which involves an interesting rhyme scheme:

> *U beating me is like a Jew becoming the next **pope**, it ain't gonna <u>happen</u>, so quit **hopin'**, 'n stop <u>rappin'</u>*

There are other good variations of this type of punch. As always, make sure you use variations if you find yourself using this type of punch more than once or twice.

> *You punching me?*
> *You're more likely to marry Jerry Fallwell*

> *The day you win is the day the Marlboro Man quits smoking*

Punchlines That Diss Your Opponents Name

This type of punchline is made popular thanks to the large number of wack / unoriginal names that emcees decide to adopt for themselves. You can easily use this type of punch when your opponent has a name involving any combination of the following: lyrical / verbal / gun / king / diety / ruler / G / chrome / gansta / doctor / killer.

Dissing someone's name is usually a must-do in online battles, and it's done a lot in live battles too since your opponents name is probably the first thing you'll learn about them. Try to use other techniques in these punches to make them strong. Here are two good examples, both of which involve wordplay. The second one plays around with "matzah," which is the bread that doesn't rise when cooked, and is eaten during Passover.

> *You don't stand a chance in this race like Hillary,*
> *Dr. Death you're not a doctor cuz u suck at delivery*

> *Gangsta Masta? more like Gangsta Matzah,*
> *You ain't rising,*
> *I'll cook ya young ass up like Gangsta Pasta*

PART FIVE
RECORDING

Setting Up a Project Studio

> **droppin' knowledge**
>
> *"Usually I get to the studio around 3 PM, and my hours can vary anywhere from two hours to, I mean, my record is 79 hours non stop. As long as the ideas are flowing, I'm in here. I feel when I come to the studio, I have the same energy today as I did 20 years ago when I started. I still feel it, I love music."* - Dr. Dre

Technology is doing some wild things to the music biz. The internet us allowing independent producers and artists to instantly share music with a large audience through sites like *Myspace*, *Youtube*, and *Soundclick*. Songs and videos can be downloaded, either for free or at low cost, making underground music more accessible than ever. The old idea that an artist can only sell CDs through a record label is dead – any artist can be heard if that artist can achieve a few simple steps.

In order to get your music out there, you have to make a decent recording. That sounds obvious, but a good recording can be the difference between people feeling your music and people covering their ears when you push play. Luckily, making good recordings is easier than ever, also thanks to technology. Because everything is recorded digitally now, it's much easier for an amateur musician or rapper to produce a fairly high quality single. Twenty years ago, you had to rent a specialized recording studio with a highly trained engineer to cut a demo. Now you can produce a radio-ready single in your bedroom. For the most part, technology has narrowed the gap between professional musicians and the rest of us.

The computer is the single most important part of the digital studio set-up and the key to all of this new technology. With a computer you can record songs, mix songs, send them off to clubs to try and book a gig, and even create a community of fans that you can tell when you have shows coming up. Of course, for those without access to a computer, the technology gap is probably getting wider. That's what social critics refer to as the 'digital divide.' Our advice to all those rappers who don't have computers is to find a way to get to one. Either save up to buy one (you can now get a really decent desktop for $500), hit up the library (free internet access), or hook up with one of your friends who does have a computer with internet access. Spitting a dope rap on a street corner is great, but the chance that a booking agent or record exec will notice you is slim. So get a computer. It makes starting out as an emcee much easier.

The Studio

So you have a friend who made this dope beat or you found one on the internet that you like, and you want to lay down vocals. If you can't afford the $100/hr at a big facility, it's no problem. Without much cost, you can set up a really decent home studio. There are 6 basic components to every home studio.

1. The Room

Professional studios always have a booth for recording vocals (sometimes called a *vocal booth* or *isolation (iso) booth*). A booth is essentially a soundproof room that helps prevent background noise (cars, air conditioners, kid brothers) from being heard on the track. Most vocal booths cost thousands of dollars because they use expensive soundproof foam and other acoustic treatments. The good news is that you don't need to build one. You can actually create a pretty isolated sound by using things you find around the house: pillows, blankets, old mattresses, etc... Ideally, you should get your computer to the quietest room in the house. Tell your roommates / parents not to bother you, close the door, stuff some towels in the windows, and tack some blankets on the walls. Once you have a good space to record, you're ready to go out and get the gear.

2. The Computer

As we said, the computer is the foundation of digital

The Studio

recording and modern music distribution. There are tons of software programs that will allow you to record and mix (we'll get to those), but in order to use that software, you need a relatively powerful computer. Here are some specs:

* You need a pretty fast processor (speeds of at least 2.0khz).
* You need a pretty big hard drive because audio files are big (go for 50gb).
* You need at least 512mb of RAM (random access memory) because most recording software is pretty tough on memory.

Other than that, the frills are optional. Our advice is that you do some research at a computer store like Best Buy, Circuit City, or CompUSA, or look online at Dell.com and HP.com. You should be able to buy a solid desktop or laptop for around $500.

3. The Microphone

Other than the computer, the microphone is the most important part of the equation because it is the device that transfers sound from your vocal chords to the track. A microphone basically converts sound to electricity in a format that can be recorded. You want that device to preserve all of the good things about your sound, while it smoothes out the not-so-good things. Professionals put most of their money into mics to get "perfect", "natural" vocal sounds. In our experience, a decent mic is enough to get you started.

There are two basic types of microphone: condenser and dynamic. Within these types, microphones can be distinguished by their frequency response and their directional pickup pattern (omni, uni, cardioid). For the most part, all you have to know is what type of mic to use in the studio and what type to use on the stage.

For most vocal recording, you want what is generally called a studio condenser microphone (also called a capacitor mic). Condenser mics are very sensitive and very fragile, so they're great for recording vocals in a quiet environment. Most condenser mics have a flat frequency response, meaning that they can accurately represent the full range of textures within the human voice. Note that most condenser mics require an external 48 volt power source (phantom power), which most audio interfaces provide.

When you take your act live, you'll probably want to go with a dynamic mic. This is the type of microphone that you've probably seen most frequently – a spherical screen on a tapered handle. These mics are known for their durability, so they're great for the demanding conditions of the stage. The downside is that they need loud signal sources to accurately represent sound and that they don't pickup much high and low frequency.

In other words, dynamic mics are not ideal in a studio where you want a nice, balanced vocal sound. The Shure SM-58 is one of the most popular dynamic stage mics. When building your studio, spring for the condenser.

Guide To Studio Mics

Extremely cheap	
Marshall Electronics MXL V57M	$60 - $70
Samson C01U USB Condenser	$80
Middle of the road	
Marshall Electronics MXL770	$90
AKG Perception 200	$160
Semi-pro	
Shure KSM 27	$300
Rode NT1000	$300
Nasty	
Neumann TLM 103	$1,000
Neumann U87Ai	$2,500
Insane (Dr. Dre's mic)	
Sony C800-G	$7,350

Any of these mics will get you started with a clean, professional sound.

4. The Audio Interface

In order to read the signal coming from your microphone, your computer needs to have a way to communicate with it. There are three ways to do this:

A. USB/Firewire interface: A free standing box with mic inputs that powers your microphone and translates the signal for the computer. A free-standing interface is best because it features several mic inputs, mic preamps that give the mics extra punch, and phantom power, which most high-quality condenser mics require. Two suggestions for general interfaces are:

Interface

M-Audio Audiophile PCI Interface (soundcard)	$99
Line6 TonePort UX2 USB Computer Recording Interface (USB)	$200

Note: some programs like ProTools require special interfaces and can not be used with the two mentioned above.

B. USB Microphone: If your budget is too small for an external interface, some manufacturers now make microphones that plug directly into your computer's

USB port (check out the Samson C01U USB Condenser above). These mics are powered by the USB cable and feed directly into your computer's recording software.

C. Computer Mic Input: Your computer will have a small input for a microphone (1/8" input), which can be used for recording. While this is the cheapest option (you can use any mic for this), there are several problems with this method including bad sound and unnecessary strain on your sound card/processor. You will also need external phantom power for most condenser mics. Also, if you go this route, you'll need an adapter to change the mic output from 1/4" to 1/8".

5. The Software

In order to make music on a computer, you need some simple software to record and display the sounds you make in the microphone. In the past few years, dozens of options have popped up, so it all comes down to your budget and what meets your needs.

There are several programs out there that let you import and display sounds in wave form, which allows you to edit your sounds. If you want more advanced features, you're going to have to pay a little more. You can find good prices on all this software at SameDayMusic.com. Here are some of the most popular options:

Software

Mackie Tracktion2 (unlimited track count)	$150
Cakewalk SONAR Home Studio XL (simple and easy)	$160
Reason (great samples and synths)	$300
Protools LE with Mbox interface (the industry standard)	$500

6. Headphones

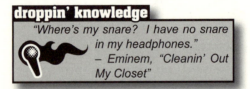

droppin' knowledge
"Where's my snare? I have no snare in my headphones."
– Eminem, "Cleanin' Out My Closet"

Now that your making music with a computer, you need a way to hear the sound while you're recording and editing. While most professional engineers use speakers (called monitors) for playback, you can get away with headphones in the short-term. Headphones allow you to listen to the track while you record and let you monitor playback while you mix. Note: Be careful with volume. Now that you're mixing music, you want to make sure you don't damage your ears by mixing with the volume too high.

The Studio

The important things about headphones are comfort and muffling. You want to make sure they feel good because you'll be wearing them a lot. You also want to make sure they muffle sound so that the track doesn't bleed into your mic while you're rapping. Here are some suggestions for headphones:

Headphones

Basic: *Behringer HPM1000* (moderate bleed)	$15
Decent: *Sennheiser HD212* (very little bleed)	$60
Pro: *AKG K271* (no bleed)	$200

The Full Package

So that's the deal with the home studio set-up. You need a computer, a microphone, an audio interface, some software, headphones, and a quiet room. Keep in mind, this outline is just the beginning of the research you should do if you're going to spend your hard-earned cash on studio gear. Our advice: go down to the music store and talk to the salespeople about everything they know.

Good studio gear is crucial for a good rapper. But good gear never made a bad rapper good. Don't neglect your rhymes.

The Full Package (on a budget)

Microphone	
Marshall Electronics MXL770	$90
Interface	
M-Audio Audiophile PCI Interface (soundcard)	$100
Software	
Mackie Tracktion 2	$150
Headphones	
Behringer HPM1000	$15
Total	
Total package	$360

ON THE MIC

droppin' knowledge

"I'm focused when I'm recording. When I record I slip into the zone. I don't like to talk a lot. I like to stick to myself and get my thoughts together, think how I'm going to map out each song. Each song is fairly easy to write.

I record vocals on one day and take the tape home to listen to them overnight. Then I do more vocals the next day. I always do my vocals twice. I might have the skeleton down, the vocals and the beat, for two months before I think of the finishing touches to put on it, like sound effects or if I want the beat to drop out here or something. I take my time." - Eminem

Spitting rhymes wither your friends is one thing, but when it comes to actually stepping to the mic to record a vocal track, that's a whole new ballgame. Whether you're spitting into your cheap computer mic at home or you're in a studio doing a guest appearance on someone's record, these tips will help you get a high-quality verse on the track.

Enunciate

While it's always important to rap clearly so that people understand what you're saying, it's more important when you're on the mic. If you're laying down some gem of a verse for all of posterity, you better not be mumbling or slurring your words (unless that's a natural part of your style). I'm not saying you have to rap like you're Brian Williams on the evening news, but you definitely want to articulate every syllable you've written. Make sure your lines are understood.

Confidence

Whatever you need to do to psych yourself up, do it. The more confidence you have, the better you're going to deliver. Whether that means you pound on your chest, meditate, call your mamma real quick, say "hell yeah!" a bunch of times, or listen to a song that pumps you up, do whatever it takes. Then rip it up.

Breath Easily

Just because you're all fired up and ready to go doesn't mean you should be screaming and yelling and then gasping for breath. Rap at a volume that lets you breath easily during pauses in your lines.

Don't Pop Your P's

A lot of emcees and singers have problems with their P's. When they pronounce the letter "P," they let their lips smack a little and this can create a pop on the track.

Thankfully, there are two solutions to this problem.

This first is a screen between you and the mic. Pop-screens are available cheaply and are an important investment if you have a condenser mic. They reduce the effect of pops and prevent your salvia from actually hitting the mic. Most music stores have a generic pop-screen for about $20. Or you can grab a slightly higher quality one: Shure makes the Popperstopper.

If you don't want to buy a pop-screen, you can build one. Just grab a wire coat hanger and a woman's stocking. Bend the coat hanger into a circle 3"- 6" wide, and then put the stocking over it and pull it tight. Then secure the coat hanger to the mic stand.

The other important trick you can do with your mouth. When saying p's or b's, instead of actually making a "pop" with your lips, let your lips touch only slightly. It's almost like you're sucking in the "p" or "b" a little. You don't have to exaggerate this too much, but a little concentration can get rid of those annoying pops.

Drink Water / Eat Mints

You can't spit rhymes without salivia. In order to keep flowing easily on a track, make sure your mouth isn't dry. I always have a big bottle of water with me when I'm on the mic, and I usually drink some or chew some mints before each verse to get the salivia flowing.

To Punch In or Not to Punch In

To "punch" or "punch in" means to start recording a verse somewhere in the middle of the verse - i.e. not starting from the beginning.

For a long time, punching in was thoroughly avoided by rappers. A rapper who couldn't spit a verse all the way through was thought to be weak or unskilled. For a long time, it was a thing of pride. The best rappers would step to the microphone, spit it all the way through once or twice, do some doubles and then be done.

The good thing about this method (other than the fact that it's impressive) is that it ensures an even pitch and good continuity throughout. The drawback to this method is that in an effort to show off how skilled you are, you might not get the best verse on the track. And if you do make mistakes, you have to start over from the beginning.

Unless you're stepping into the booth with Jay-Z watching, there's really no need to spit all the way through. Flow for as long as you can without losing your breath or messing up. Then punch in somewhere that makes sense. You want the track to sound continuous, so try to match your pitch and tone.

Doubling

Doubling vocals means laying a second vocal track on top of the first to emphasize certain words or phrases. Most rappers utilize this technique to add depth and texture to their verses. Here are three techniques.

Standard doubles. The way most rappers double is to let the track play and occasionally spit a few words or lines on top of the original. This way they can emphasize the words they want, and let the rest of the lines stand on their own. One big problem a lot of amateur's have is that they don't match the pitch and tone of their original verse and so the double sounds sloppy. Try to match your tone as you double. Avoid always doubling just the rhymes at the end of bars.

Tupac-style doubles. Tupac often employed a technique of doubling himself throughout a verse on almost every line to add intensity to the whole track. Depending on your voice, this technique can work very well or very poorly. The key is to make sure your voice and flow are identical the second time as they were the first time. If you can't get them to match up exactly, avoid this type of double.

No doubles. Some of the best verses out there don't have doubles. When you listen to certain Kanye, Jay-Z, or Big Daddy Kane, they don't have doubles and the verses sound tight. Not every verse needs doubles.

PART SIX
THE MOTIVATION BEHIND YOUR RHYMES

WHY SPIT RHYMES

If you've gotten this far, chances are you have some personal reasons why you're learning to spit lyrical swords. But in case you're having second thoughts, here are the top 5 reasons you should learn to rap.

1. To Express Yourself

Rapping is a form of self-expression like writing poetry or painting. Every emcee is an artist, and his rhymes are his art. Whether you spit raps for other people or not, writing rhymes about your life and your thoughts is a great way to express yourself and get things off your chest. It's a way to share some of your ideas, feelings and thoughts with other people. It's a good way to build confidence. I know guys who were scared to talk in high school until they built up their confidence freestyling. It's like Rakim says in this alliteration-rich lyric: "self esteem make me super superb and supreme." Express yourself and build up your confidence.

2. To Make Money Someday

Nobody's promising you anything. Just because you pick up a microphone or spit a couple of bars in a cipher doesn't mean if you drop an album anyone other than your mom is going to buy it. But if you're seriously dedicated to the art form, if you're committed to studying the techniques in-depth, and if you're willing to practice until your gums bleed, then you have a much better chance of eventually creating some music that people will listen to. Thankfully, technology has made getting into the rap game easier than ever. You might not go pro, but there are lots of talented emcees who don't rap full time (they have other jobs), but they do shows and sell mixtapes, and have a good thing going on.

3. To Get Smarter

Freestyling makes you smarter. It's as simple as that. Freestyle rapping is a highly demanding cognitive task that requires you to think about rhyming words and their meaning all in a manner of milliseconds. You won't develop the enormous memory of a spelling bee champion, or the ability to think about space the way a chess master can, but you'll be able to think on your feet as well as anyone in the world. In case you're interested, you'll develop the kind of thinking abilities that will help you from getting Alzheimers later on in life. Plus, in order to improve as a rapper, you will be improving your vocabulary, your writing ability, and your knowledge of current events and history.

4. To Get People's Attention / Respect

Spitting a dope freestyle rap is definitely one of the easiest ways to get people's attention. Whether you're trying to be more popular at school, or you want to impress that girl / guy you work with, kicking a freestyle is the way to do it. It's also a perfect way to meet people at bars or parties. Just find someone you can spit with and then go wild. You can battle if you want, or you can just cipher. Before you know it, a circle with gather around you, and you'll be more popular than American Idol. That's a promise.

5. To Have Fun

Rapping should be fun. Especially freestyling. Freestyling should be about being creative and having fun. Of course, there's always hard work involved; just makes sure that when it comes time to actually spit or freestyle, you're having a good time.

THE CURE FOR WRITER'S BLOCK

> **droppin' knowledge**
>
> "The beautiful thing about hip-hop is it's like an audio collage. You can take any form of music and do it in a hip-hop way and it'll be a hip-hop song. That's the only music you can do that with."
> - Talib Kweli

Rapping is an art form

One thing I love about hip-hop music that a lot of haters (and even a lot of closed minded rappers) don't understand is that rap music is a form of art. It's an art form based on borrowing elements from other forms, and using them in new ways. Think of the first DJ's who took James Brown and Parliment records and found the hidden break beats in them. DJing itself is an artform of taking something that already exists, and using it in a new way, cutting, splicing and scratching. Obviously, there is no single 'hip-hop sound.' When Afrika Bambatta was presiding over block parties in the Bronx in the late seventies, he'd instruct the DJ's to find break beats in all kinds of music, from jazz records to funk to soul to gospel to the 'beach blanket' pop songs all the white kids were listening to in the fifties. All of this got incorporated into hip-hop.

Rapping itself is a form of art. Rap is poetry, a form of verbal artistic expression. Because of this, you can rap to express anything. There are no boundaries on what rap is or can be.

When the Cold Crush Brothers spit raps at a party, no one said, "no that's what rap is supposed to be." When Public Enemy made rap political, no one said, "no, that ain't rap." When Common rapped about the emotional toll of deciding to have an abortion with his girlfriend, nobody said "that's not appropriate for rap music." When Eminem rapped about how he hates his mom, nobody said "rap isn't about that." When I wrote a song about the revolutionary war, nobody told me "rap music shouldn't be teaching history." Push the envelope. Express yourself and be real. Innovate.

What not to spit about

This is a hard lesson for a lot of young wannabe gangstas to learn: don't fake something you're not. There's nothing sadder in the whole world than a 12 year old suburbanite rapping about sippin' Crys, sittin' in the 'Lac, bustin' gats, countin' cash, pimps n' hoes. Everybody knows that you're not a gangster, pimp, murderer, drug dealer, big baller, millionaire or prison inmate. You don't have a rack of gats or a briefcase of cash, you didn't have sex with two models last night, you don't rock glocks in your tube socks and pull 'em out to just drop cops, you don't have any gold records

WRITER'S BLOCK

on your wall. You don't know what you're talking about. You might as well be rapping about what it feels like to give birth.

Just because you're rapping, doesn't mean you have to spit the same things Jay-Z spits. Unless you grew up in the Marcy Projects, were abandoned by your father as a kid, and dropped out of high school to sell crack (like he did), don't rap about it. He's rapping about his life. You rap about yours.

The other thing regards women / gay people / and some minorities. Just because you're rapping, that doesn't mean you have an excuse to be racist, sexist or homophobic. If that's how you are in real life, then that's your problem to deal with. But if you're a sensible person who doesn't hate other people just because they fall into a category that you're not in, don't spit that idiocy in your raps. Be real, and respect other people.

droppin' knowledge
*"While you talk about b*tches and switches and
hoes and clothes and weed,
let's talk about time travelin',
rhyme javelin,
something mind unravelin'"*
- Andre (3000),
"Return of the G"

What to Spit About

> **droppin' knowledge**
>
>
>
> *"I feel like too few emcees speak from their gut - it's almost all cerebral. When I'm listening to music, I want to **feel** the cat talking to me, you know? I don't want to just hear a message; that cool... but when I **feel** what's behind the message, then you got me!"* – Reconcile of Mass Reality

As Wikipedia notes, "delivery and wordplay can be indicative of a rapper's skill, but the subject of a rap is equally, if not more significant. A rapper who has an excellent delivery but lacks substance is frequently perceived as less skillful than a mediocre rapper who has a message or story." Determining the lyrical content of your music is a crucial decision that some emcees don't spend enough time considering. Certainly give the subject of your rap as much time and consideration that you give the techniques you use. Almost every artist who comes with amazing metaphors but spits about absolutely nothing is destined for total obscurity. Give it thought, and know that the possibilities are limitless.

Sometimes, though, with limitless possibilities comes unending frustration. Writer's block sets in and nothing you write seems to work. You begin to criticize your own ideas as too stupid, too obvious, or too corny. Hours pass, days pass, and you're writing nothing. Is this the end of your illustrious rap career?

Here are just a few basic ideas to get you out of that writer's block:

Rap about things around you

If you're sitting in your car freeing with a friend, rap about the streetlight out of your window, the fact that you're car doesn't have AC but it's a hot summer night, the view, what you're wearing, what people walking on the sidewalk are probably doing.

Rap about your life

Rap about what you did that day. What happened at school, at your job, in your house. Rap about how Julio came over to play X-box and told you that his sister has a crush on you. Rap about what you ate for dinner. *I mean the macaroni's soggy, the peas all mush and the chicken tastes like wood.*

Rap about impressions / frustrations / feelings

Look within yourself for inspiration. Past the surface we all have a well of energy, and you can turn that energy into creativity. Look deep. Rap about what you truly love and what you truly hate. What's making you pissed off in your life? Rap about your boss who treats you unfairly. Rap about your teacher who always favors the jocks in your class. Rap about how mad you are that your girlfriend / boyfriend just broke up with you. What's making you truly happy? Rap about getting up before everyone else and having the house to yourself. Rap about hitting that shot, getting that raise, meeting that person. Rap about your relationship.

Rap about politics / society

Rap about the social world around you. Rap about the president. Read the newspaper and then rap about the wall we're building on the border with Mexico or the bird flu, or the war in Iraq. That's realness. Like Mos Def says, "beef is not what Jay said to Nas / beef is when working ni**as can't find jobs." Rap about history.

Rap about something no one's ever rapped before

Push the envelope. Get innovative and provocative. Rap about birds. Rap about comic books. Rap about Starbucks or MLK. Rap about ancient Egypt or modern Tokyo. Rap about what it feels like to take a bath.

Tell stories in rap

Some of the great raps out there are story raps. Any story that you can tell someone, you can also tell in rap. Tell the one about getting beat up by some punks, the one about that crazy ball game, the one about going fishing with your dad.

Flow without criticizing yourself

Don't let your conscious mind censor your inner beast. Do this exercise, which was invented by the surrealists in France a hundred years ago: write without stopping, hardly thinking, barely pausing. Just write nonstop. Flow and flow and flow. Rhyme and rhyme and rhyme. Kick a freeverse. Sort through the garbage later on.

Diversify

Make every rap you spit be different from the last one you spit. Take Kanye West's first album, "The College Dropout" for example. Each song on the album addresses a topic that he cares about. Each song is unique, and it makes the album that much more listenable. Here are the topics the songs deal with:

*Family reunions ("Family Business")
*The aftermath of a car crash ("Through the Wire")
*Dropping out of school ("School Spirit")
*Jesus ("Jesus Walks")
*Working out ("The New Workout Plan")
*Insecurities ("All Falls Down")
*Getting high ("Get Em High")
*Working a crappy job ("Spaceship")

The album features those songs, plus a bunch of standard tracks just uppin' himself. And that's all on one album. There really is no limit to what you spit about. It might sound trite, but don't follow the leader, follow your passions.

> "Redundancy is what kills countless mainstream and underground Emcees. Although they do not realize it, they have repeated their message and/or style numerous times and people eventually get bored with hearing it." - Anonymous

Borrow Lines from Rakim

Finally, if all else fails and you're still hitting your head against the wall because you still can't think of any good topic for that new track you're working on, just do what all the pros do when they face writer's block: steal some lines from Rakim.

Now, this isn't actually stealing. It's not biting. With Rakim, everyone knows you're doing it because you love and revere him and respect his influence on hip-hop. Plus, his songs are a near endless source of poetic lyrics flowed with ease over bangin' beats. His lyrics will inspire. So, don't bite a whole verse, but use one of his rhymes (or the rhymes of one of your other favorite emcees) and use those as your hook. Build the rest of your song around the meaning in those lines.

Just look how great this technique worked for Mos Def, Eminem, and Talib Kweli. Here's lyrics from Rakim's , "You Know I Got Soul," used verbatim as the hook in Mos Def's "Love."

Writer's Block

> *I start to think and then I sink into the paper,*
> *like I was ink, when I'm writing I'm trapped in*
> *between the lines,*
> *I escape when I finish the rhyme*

Eminem took the following lyrics from "And the Rhyme Goes On," and reworked them for the hook in his "The Way I Am":

> *I'm the R – A – to the K – I – M,*
> *and if I wasn't then why would I say I am*

became:

> *'Cause I am whatever you say I am,*
> *and if I wasn't then why would I say I am*

Talib Kweli used these Rakim lyrics as his hook in "fortified live." The orginal song is "Follow the Leader":

> *In this journey, you're the journal, I'm the journalist*
> *Am I eternal, or an eternalist?*

So one solution to writer's block is to use the inspiration of your hip-hop predecessors as creative fuel.

When to Write

As practice is really the key to improving, you should be rapping as much as you can. One great thing about writing rhymes is that you don't have to do it outloud, so you can be writing while wating in line, while on the subway, in the elevator, on a plane, whatever. Keep a pen and a small notebook with you at all times to write down some of the rhymes you come up with. If you want to keep it hi-tech by using your Sidekick or Blackberry or whatever, do that. Sometimes, if I don't have a pad with me and I think of some good lines, I'll call myself and leave a voice message of me spitting the lines and then I'll write them down later.

There are moments too, when you'll feel the flow. You'll get in the zone and the words will come spilling out of you, metaphors, wordplay, vocabulary, multies, in-rhymes and all. Those are the amazing moments, and they happen to those who have worked hard to attain a certain level of mastery. It's the same feeling that a basketball player gets when he just can't miss. Time slows down and the basket just seems to be calling for the ball. There will be moments when your pen or your vocal chords or your fingers on the computer will just takeover and you'll watch as they deliver you line after line of beautiful rhymes.

As Rakim himself mentions, "at certain times, it's just time to write, and it flows the way I want it to flow. It's almost like I get numb and it just happens." Those are the moments that all the hard work helps you achieve. And it's worth it.

Discography

Eric B and Rakim, "Follow the Leader," *Follow the Leader*, Uni, 1988

Kanye West, "The New Workout Plan," *The College Dropout*, Roc-A-Fella, 2004

Eminem, *8-Mile*, Dir. Curtis Hanson, Universal Pictures, 2002

Jay-Z, "Encore," *The Black Album*, Roc-A-Fella / Def Jam, 2003

Classified, "Just the Way It Is," unreleased.

Kool Moe Dee, "I Go to Work," *Knowledge is King*, Jive, 1989

Mos Def, "Travellin Man," *Travellin Man*, Relativity, 1998

Eric B and Rakim, "I Know You Got Soul", *Paid in Full*, 4th and Broadway, 1987

Nas, "N.Y. State of Mind," *Illmatic*, Columbia, 1994

2Pac, "Changes," *Greatest Hits*, Interscope, 1998

Grandmaster Flash and the Furious Five, "The Message," *The Message*, Sugar Hill, 1982

Dead Prez, "Hell Yeah (Pimp the System)", *RBG: Revolutionary But Gangsta*, Sony, 2004

The Roots (Black Thought), "The Next Movement", *Things Fall Apart*, MCA, 1999

Flocabulary (Akir), "I Want America," *Hip-Hop U.S. History*, Cider

Mill, 2006

Dizzee Rascal, "Stand Up Tall," *Showtime*, XL, 2004

Ludacris, "Number One Spot," *The Red Light District*, Def Jam, 2004

D12 (Eminem), "My Band," *D12 World*, Shady / Interscope, 2004

Eminem, "The Real Slim Shady," *The Marshall Mathers LP*, Interscope, 2000

Eminem, "Lose Yourself," *8-Mile Soundtrack*, Universal, 2002

Papoose, "Thug Connection," *Thug Connection*, Select, 1999

Black Star (Punchline), "Twice Inna Lifetime," *Black Star*, Royalty, 1998

Black Star (Wordsworth), "Twice Inna Lifetime," *Black Star*, Royalty, 1998

Little Brother (Legacy), "Flash and Flare," *The Chitlin Circuit*, Fastlife, 2005

Tonedeff (Session), "Quotables," *Archetype*, Freshchest, 2005

The Roots (Black Thought), "Mellow My Man," *Do you Want More?!!!??!*, DGC, 1995

Fugees (Lauryn Hill), "How Many Mics," *The Score*, Ruffhouse, 1996

BlackStar (Talib Kweli), "Hater Players," *BlackStar*, Royalty, 1998

Common, "1-9-9-9," *Soundbombing* (compilation), Priority, 1999

DISCOGRAPHY

Canibus, "100 Bars," *2000 B.C.*, Uptown/Universal, 2000

Tonedeff, "Heavyweights," *Archetype*, Freshchest, 2005

Tonedeff (Substantial), "Quotables," *Archetype*, Freshchest, 2005

A Tribe Called Quest (Busta Rhymes), "Scenario," *Low End Theory*, Jive, 1991

Jay-Z (Bun B), "Big Pimpin," *Vol 3: Life and Times of S. Carter*, Roc-A-Fella, 1999

OutKast (Andre 3000), "Wheelz of Steel," *ATLiens*, LA Face, 1996

Papoose, "That's a Good Look," Unrealesed

Talib Kweli (Papoose), "The Beast," *Right About Now*, Koch, 2005

Tupac, "Let Knowledge Drop" *The Lost Tapes*, Lightyear, 2000

Talib Kweli and Hi Tek (Raw Digga), "Down for the Count," *Reflection Eternal*,
Priority, 2000

BlackStar (Talib Kweli), "Thieves in the Night," *BlackStar*, Royalty, 1998

Immortal Technique, "The Point of Now Return," *Revolutionary, Vol. 2*, Viper, 2003

Jay-Z, "Hovi Baby," *The Blueprint 2*, Roc-a-fella, 2002

Aesop Rock, "Oxygen," *Float*, Mush, 1999

Cormega, "Rap's a Hustle," *The Realness*, Landscape, 2001

Eminem, "Any Man," Unreleased

Eminem, "My Dad's Gone Crazy," *The Eminem Show*, Interscope, 2002

OutKast (Raekwon the Chef), "Skew it on the Bar-B," *Aquemini*, LA Face, 1998

Kanye West (Consequence), "Gone," *Late Registration*, Roc-A-Fella, 2005

Chamillionaire, "Riding Dirty," Single, 2006

2Pac, "Hit Em Up," *Greatest Hits*, Death Row, 1998

Eminem, "Kill Whitey," Unreleased

Dead Prez, "It's Bigger than Hip-Hop," *Let's Get Free*, Relativity, 2000

Jay-Z, "Moment of Clarity," *The Black Album*, Roc-A-Fella / Def Jam, 2003

Sugarhill Gang, "Rapper's Delight," *Rapper's Delight*, Sugarhill, 1980

Grandmaster Flash and Furious Five, "The Message," The Message, Sugar Hill, 1982

Eric B. and Rakim, "I Ain't No Joke," *Paid in Full*, 4th and Broadway, 1987

Notorious B.I.G., "Hypnotize," *Life After Death*, Bad Boy, 1997

Eminem, "Cleanin Out My Closet," *The Eminem Show*, Interscope, 2002

Outkast, "So Fresh, So Clean," *Stankonia*, LaFace / Arista, 2000

The Coup, "Pimps," *Genocide and Juice*, Wild Pitch, 1994

KRS-One, "You Gon Go" *Keep Right*, Grit, 2004

OutKast, "Return of the G," *Aquemini*, LA Face, 1998

Mos Def, "Love," *Black on Both Sides,* Rawkus, 1999

Eminem, "The Way I Am," *The Marshall Mathers LP*, Interscope, 2000

Talib Kweli, "Fortified Live," *Soundbombing* (compilation), Royalty, 1997

Sources

Wordsworth as quoted in "Wordsworth: An Emcee Wealthy in Words" by Todd E Jones aka New Jeru Poet, *HipHop-Elements*, Jan 3, 2005.
Hiphop-elements.com

The American Heritage Dictionary of the English Language, Fourth Edition, Houghton Mifflin Company, 2000.
Dictionary.com

Sage Francis as quoted in "Sage Francis: Concrete Abstractions" by Jason Pepe, *Zero Magazine,* January, 2005.
ZeroMag.com

Bun B as quoted in the "Bun B" by Jon Caramanica, *The Believer Magazine*, June – July, 2006.
Believermag.com

Immortal Technique as quoted in "Immortal Technique: Rock the Boat" by Brendan Frederick, *XXL*, Wednesday, April 5th, 2006.
xxlmag.com

Skillz as quoted in "Skillz: The Will of a Ghostwriter" by Chris Yuscavage, *AllHipHop.com*.
AllHipHop.com

Ludacris as quoted in "Hip-Hop Fridays: Exclusive Q & A With Ludacris," by Cedric Muhammad, *BlackElectorate.com*, May 09, 2003.
BlackElectorate.com

Tonedeff as quoted in interview by Sumo Kaplunk, *Original UK Hip-Hop*, September 29, 2004.
Ukhh.com

Rakim as quoted in "Status Ain't Hood Interviews Rakim" by Tom Breihan, *The Village Voice*, June 6, 2006.

Jin as quoted in interview by Daz, *Zen Nation*, March 3, 2003.
Zennation.com

Dre. Dre as quoted in "Interview with Dre," *Scratch Magazine*, Issue 7 Sept / Oct 2005.
Scratchmagazine.com

Eminem as quoted in "Oh Yes, It's Shady's Night," Eminem.net, April 28, 2000.
Eminem.net

Talib Kweli as quoted on Brainyquote.com.
Brainyquote.com

Frida Kahlo's painting is Autorretrato Con Pelo Suelto, 1947 (private collection).

Appendix 1 - List of Idioms for Wordplay

Here is a list of idioms you can use to create wordplay in your rhymes. Each phrase below has a literal meaning and an idiomatic meaning, so you create wordplay by 'playing' with these two meanings. In reverse alphabetical order:

You are what you eat
X marks the spot
Wolf in sheep's clothing
Whole nine yards
Wag the dog
Up a creek with no paddle
(or up sh**'s creek with no paddle)
Turn a blind eye
'Til the cows come home
There's more than one way to skin a cat
The straw that broke the camel's back
The harder they come, the harder they fall
Tie the knot
Third world
Son of gun
Straight from the horse's mouth
Spitting Image
Southpaw
Sour grapes
Sleep tight
Skin of your teeth
Shot in the dark
Shake a leg

Scapegoat
Saved by the bell
Rule of thumb
Rain cats and dogs
Rain check
Put your best foot forward
Put on your thinking cap
Put a sock in it
Push the envelope
Pull out all the stops
Pull the wool over your eyes
Pull the plug
Pedal to the metal
Pardon my French
Over the top
Off the record
Off the cuff
Off the top
Not playing with a full deck
No dice
New York minute
New kid on the block
My dogs are barking
Mum's the word
Make no bones about it
Mad as a hatter
Loose cannon
Level playing field
Know the ropes
Knock on wood
Knee jerk reaction
Kick the bucket

APPENDIX I - IDIOMS

Keep your chin up
I wash my hands of it
Ivy League
In your face
In the bag
I'll have your head on a platter
Houston, we have a problem
Honeymoon
Hold your horses
Hit the hay
High five
Hell in a hand basket
Heavy metal
Hat trick
Graveyard shift
Go the extra mile
Go out on a limb
Gild the lily
French kiss
Foam at the mouth
Fly on the wall
Flip the bird
Flea market
Field day
Feeding frenzy
Face the music
Eat, drink and be merry
Eighty-sixed
Dry run
Drinks like a fish
Dropping like flies
Drop dime

Drag Race
Double Whammy
Don't look a gift horse in the mouth
Dog days
Dirt poor
Diamond in the rough
Devil's advocate
Dead ringer
Deadline
Cup of Joe
Cut to the chase
Cut to the quick
Cock and bull story
Cold war
Close but no cigar
Chow down
Chip on his shoulder
Charley horse
Caught with your pants down
Bullpen
Brownie points
Break a leg
Blind leading the blind
Blackmail
Big apple
Balls to the wall
Ball and chain
Baker's dozen
Back to square one
Back to basics
Apple of my eye
An axe to grind

Appendix II - Rhyming with Famous People

Using slant rhyme, we can build long mulites that rhyme with the names of various celebrities. Post your own on the Flocab Rhyme Boards.

George Bush - more mush, pork hooves, horse tush,
Britney Spears - sing me cheers, rickety stairs, bring me beers
John Kerry - mom's chevy, farmer's ready, Tom Petty
P Diddy - he's silly, cheesily, feasibly
Johnny Damon - Boston hates him, mommy makes 'em
Bill Gates - still hates, forty ill dates, foibles
Pope Benedict the 16th - I scope derelicts who bring beef, I know heavyweights who fix teeth
Dick Cheney - quick ain't he?, it's rainy
50 Cent - nifty pants, hippy-man, sixty cent
Napolean - grab hold of him, my flow is thin, fallopian
Kobe Bryant - Oh, she's trying, scope these tyrants, hope he's lying
Ashlee Simpson - wacky ish son, mad we whipped 'em, one size fits 'em
Colonel Sanders - infernal chambers, herbal dandruff

Apendix III - Rhyming with Rhymeless Words

There are many words that have no rhyme in the English language, "orange" is only the most famous. But just because these words have no 'perfect rhyme' doesn't mean we can't rhyme with them. Using slant rhyme, we can rhyme with these words anyway.

Orange - lozenge, boring, forage, porridge, door-hinge
Silver - filter, shiver, filler, deliver, liver
Purple - Steve Urkel, whirlpool, urinal
Month - dunce, hunts, moth, runt
Ninth - mine, lines, absinth, labyrinth
Pint - ain't, paint, might
Wolf - gulf, fur, enough, dull
Opus - flow this, rope is, Lupus, lotus, bogus, psychosis
Dangerous - onerous, cameras, game to us, spontaneous
Marathon - care what's on, dandruff song, Dara's wrong, Santa's con
Discombobulate - the disco they love to hate, Crisco ovulate, risky even on a date, Sisqo's rollerblades

RAP ONLINE

You can freestyle, drop written rhymes and compete in topical competitions on the Flocab Rhyme Boards.
www.flocabulary.com/board

You can battle and freestyle on Emcee Battle Forum.
www.emceebattleforum.com

ABOUT FLOCABULARY

Flocabulary is committed to promoting literacy through positive hip-hop music. Founded by Alex Rappaport and Blake Harrison in 2004, Flocabulary continues to produce books, CD's, and dynamic live shows. Flocabulary is based in New York City. Check out www.flocabulary.com for more information.